When Steelworkers Defined Chicago

How Chicago-Gary Area Steelworkers Led the U.S. Industrial Union Movement

Doug Nelson

Steelworkers History Project

Chicago

First Edition

Library of Congress Control Number: 2025922683

The paper used in this publication meets the minimum requirements of the American National Standard for Information Sciences – Permanence of Paper for Printed Library Materials, ANSI Z39.48-1992.

Steelworkers History Project

info@steelworkershistory.org

Chicago, Illinois

This book is dedicated to all the past members of Local 1033 of the United Steelworkers. Local 1033 represented proud union members who worked at Republic Steel/LTV Steel on Chicago's South Side. I had the honor of being elected to union leadership by the Local's members. It was a privilege serving them, and I made lifelong friendships.

Doug Nelson

Preface

Why study labor history? Many retired union members worry that today's generation takes things for granted. And perhaps they do. I help teach classes that introduce manufacturing concepts to young people, and many of them barely know what manufacturing is, let alone what a union does.

We need to understand the struggles of the past. Why? Because it is human nature that economic and political forces will take advantage of those who are not educated, organized, or do not know how to organize. If the union movement has taught nothing else, it teaches that the most effective way to make gains is for people to act in an organized manner.

The Steelworkers Union (USW) in the Chicago-Gary area has a proud history. There were many attempts to organize in the steel industry before the union finally took hold.The accomplishments by Chicago-Gary steelworkers have led not only steelworkers nationwide but also other unions in industrial America. Young people and others need to study the contributions of generations of union activists to building a nation and democratizing its often brutal workplaces. It is also essential to study the struggles for democracy in the union itself. It is an important lesson for people to understand that we can't just stand back and say, 'Let the leaders lead. 'Without a process to hold leaders accountable, leaders will inevitably lose touch with rank-and-file members. This has happened at times in the past with the Steelworkers Union, as well as other parts of organized labor.

This book is intended to be a readable, popular-style history while including the most relevant material. It is not intended to be an academic study, so I have omitted footnotes and complete references. I have identified the material I relied on in the reference section for those who wish to read more detailed and scholarly accounts of the chapter subjects.

I wish to thank the many people for their help at various points in putting this book together.

I want to thank fellow union officials at former USWA Local 1033 for their comments and help on the project. They include Jerry Novak, Pete O'Day, Frank Pokrywczynski, Ted Stalnos, and Victor Storino.

I want to thank the members of the Ed Sadlowski family for their help with source material and for their other comments. They include his children, Edward Sadlowski Jr., former Alderwoman Sue Sadlowski Garza, and his grandson Dave Garza.

I would like to thank Ed Sadlowski's campaign manager, Edgar James, for his invaluable assistance with the campaign's comments.

I would like to thank James Lane and Mike Olzanski, the editors of a history that compiled interviews and original material on the Sadlowski campaign, from which

I have quoted. Their work is cited in the Chapter Reference Material.

I want to thank everyone who took the time to be interviewed. That includes the invaluable assistance of former USWA District 31 Director Jack Parton; President Bill Alexander of the former USWA Local 1657; former USWA Local 65 officials Mark Collins and Lupe Valdez; former USWA Local 1010 official Joe Rodriguez; and William Kornblum.

I also thank the employees of the Chicago History Museum and the reference library of Indiana University, NW.I want to especially thank the Southeast Chicago Historical Society and its Museum at Calumet Park in Chicago.

Doug Nelson

Chicago, Illinois

November, 2025

Abbreviations Used

AA	Amalgamated Association of Iron, Steel, and Tin Workers
AFL	American Federation of Labor
CIO	Congress of Industrial Organizations
DPC	Dues Protest Committee
ENA	Experimental Negotiating Agreement
HRC	Human Relations Committee
IWW	International Workers of the World
MFD	Miners for Democracy
NLRA	National Labor Relations Act
NLRB	National Labor Relations Board
SUB	Supplemental Unemployment Benefit
SWOC	Steel Workers Organizing Committee
UAW	United Auto Workers
UMW	United Mine Workers
USWA	United Steelworkers of America (before 2005)
USW	United Steel Workers (2005 and after)
WSB	Wage Stabilization Board

Table of Contents

Introduction

The mass production of steel began in the United States during the 1870s.It started in the Pittsburgh area but quickly expanded to the Chicago area. Since that time, the American steel industry has gone back and forth between being heavily unionized and hardly organized at all. It was highly unionized until the Homestead strike of 1892, almost entirely nonunion from 1892 until U.S. Steel recognized the Steelworkers Organizing Committee in 1937, and highly unionized again from 1937 until steel production capacity began to disappear in the late 1970s.At present, much of the steel industry, such as the 'mini-mills,' is unorganized. Significant steel strikes have marked periods of both union growth and decline.

As the steel industry has been transformed, so has the union. Initially, the union organization was purely among skilled workers in the steel industry. Now the official name of the United Steelworkers is the United Steel, Paper and Forestry, Rubber, Manufacturing, Energy, Allied Industrial and Service Workers International Union. Its members range from not only steel industry workers, but also graduate students working for colleges, and almost every other occupation.

How was this union formed? In 1918, at the end of World War I, working conditions in the steel industry were harsh. Wages were low, and most men had to work 12-hour shifts seven days a week. On Sundays, they would change shifts and work a 24-hour day. In addition, safety was nonexistent. Death rates and serious injuries were extremely high.

Fast forward 50 years to 1968. Workers in United States steel mills were the highest-paid industrial workers in the world. They had excellent benefits, including first-class medical insurance, extended vacations, supplemental pay if laid off, and pensions, which provided a livable retirement.

How did the standard of living for workers in the steel industry rise so far and so fast? It was primarily due to a union which became the largest and most powerful industrial union in the country – the United Steelworkers. The union was not the only reason for success. Labor laws passed by Congress and occasional interventions by politicians of both parties helped at critical times. But without the Union at the core, nothing else would have really changed conditions.

This book will cover the formation of the union in the Chicago-Gary area and its successes and failures along the way. The union led other unions across the country as they tried to organize and advance.

Chapter 1 Steel Comes to Chicago. The Amalgamated Association of Iron, Steel, and Tin Workers (AA), the first national union to include steel workers, was formed in 1876 after winning a series of local labor battles across steelmaking areas of Pennsylvania and Ohio. The union's strength, however, was in the iron industry. As iron manufacturers began to switch to steel production during the 1880s, skilled ironworkers fought to maintain their control over production. Many manufacturers switched from iron to steel by closing their iron plants and opening up new steel mills with less-skilled, nonunion workers. This led to the battle between early union organizers and the industry at Carnegie Steel's Homestead works in Pennsylvania. At the time, Homestead was the leading steelworks in the U.S. The AA represented skilled workers at the mill and was met with violence from Carnegie that made this one of the most famous battles in American labor history. Afterward, the union had a generation of defeats in its attempts to organize.

By the early 1900s, the industry was almost completely nonunion. After World War I, a great strike wave broke out. Workers had been limited in their ability to get wage increases during the war, and in 1919, workers in many industries, including steel, struck their employers. The Great Steel Strike, as it was known, started in the Chicago mills and quickly spread to the rest of the mills in the Pittsburgh area. For many reasons, this strike was lost, and steel companies reacted with a vengeance during the 1920s. Mills were almost completely nonunion until the end of the Great Depression.

Chapter 2The Union is Forged is about the successful battle to organize the steel industry in the Chicago area and elsewhere. The Depression in the 1930s caused much economic hardship but provided opportunities for organizing. Labor laws were passed, and a major industrial labor organization – the Congress of Industrial Organizations (CIO) – was formed. This led to the creation of the Steel Worker Organizing Committee. An early victory came when the giant of the industry, U.S. Steel, agreed to recognize the union without a fight. Then came the real battle. The seven steel companies known as Little Steel, led by Republic Steel, refused to negotiate. This led to the Memorial Day Massacre and related deaths across the country. The union won final recognition in 1942 by the steel industry after the U.S. entered World War II.

Chapter 3 Fighting to Preserve Gains covers the period after World War II, when the union had to fight to consolidate its wage gains and negotiate for benefits and working conditions. The Union made a transition from its first President, Philip Murray, to David McDonald. McDonald focused on increasing contract benefits such as pensions, health care, and supplements to unemployment pay. He provided the framework for the modern contract that the steelworkers have today. The largest union strike in U.S. history occurred in 1959 as the union defended work rules on manning in the mills. The industry began to see threats from imported steel and other materials being used as steel substitutes.

Chapter 4, **Union Rebellion,** is about how the Union has reacted to opposition within its ranks. The

Steelworkers Union is structurally the most democratic labor union in the United States. All of its top officers, convention delegates, and local union officials are elected by the members. Countering that structure is the reality that John L. Lewis originally staffed the new union with Mine Worker officials and ran it as a top-down organization. The International Union has not always reacted to union democracy well. In 1959, Congress passed the Landrum-Griffith Act, and though it had an anti-union motivation, it gave rank-and-file union members a 'Bill of Rights'. The civil rights movement in the 1960s led to the Ad Hoc Committee from the Chicago mills, which fought for rights in the International Union. The union had a series of dissenters in national elections, and it culminated in one of the most exciting election campaigns in American labor history. Most of these movements started or were joined by members in the Chicago District. The Chicago-Gary District Director, Edward Sadlowski, ran for International President against St. Louis District Director Lloyd McBride, who was favored by most of the Pittsburgh union establishment. This was a campaign where Sadlowski promoted greater union democracy, including the right of the membership to vote on their contracts. Sadlowski did not win the election, but many of his ideas were incorporated into the union by leaders like Jack Parton, who followed him.

Chapter 5 New Challenges New Dircctions is the present period. The industry has undergone restructuring from deep losses in the 1980s. There were betrayals like the failed rail mill proposal at Southworks and the bitter six-month lockout by USX in 1986. Mini-mills, most of which are nonunion, are complete with full-scale steel mills. Mini-mills use recycled scrap steel and do not have the 'legacy' costs major steel mills have. The Union has undergone similar restructuring. It must change to survive the new economy. The Union and industry have, in contract bargaining, experimented with participatory work teams with mixed results. Both the companies and union officials often find it easier to do things 'the old way'. Former USW President Lynn Williams created "New Directions" bargaining goals. It has changed labor relations at some companies in many positive ways. Will it last?

1 Steel Comes to Chicago

Illinois Steel c.a. 1900

The beginnings of the steel industry in Chicago can be traced back to the mid-19th century, with the city's first rail-rolling mill, the North Chicago Rolling Mill Company, located along the North Branch of the Chicago River and opened in 1857.

By 1860, when it employed about 200 men and manufactured nearly $700,000 worth of iron railroad rails, the plant was one of the largest manufacturing enterprises in the Chicago region. In 1865, the mill rolled a few experimental steel rails, which may have been the first ever produced in the United States. In the early 1870s, when it employed about 1,500 men, the company added a Bessemer furnace, enabling it to produce steel rails in large quantities. At the beginning of the 1880s, the company opened a large new plant in South Chicago that also made steel rails. By the mid-1880s, the two mills together employed about 6,000 people and produced over 600,000 tons annually. In 1889, the two plants of the North Chicago Rolling Mill Co. became the heart of the new Illinois Steel Co., an entity that merged several of the largest Chicago-area mills into what was then the world's largest steel company. At the beginning of the twentieth century, Illinois Steel became part of U.S. Steel.

Chicago Becomes the Nation's Industrial Center

Steel making marked a shift in Chicago's metalworking landscape, which had previously consisted primarily of smaller iron foundries. This marked the beginning of significant industrial development, driven by the city's geographical advantages and the ready availability of raw materials. Chicago's steel industry grew to become the largest in the nation, with one mill, U.S. Steel Southworks, producing more steel than Great Britain.

Workers going into Illinois Steel

(Later U.S. Steel Southworks) at the Chicago 89th Street gate in the early 1900s

Several factors contributed to Chicago's rise as a steel production center:

- Strategic location: Situated on the Great Lakes and near the Calumet River, Chicago offered excellent transportation routes for bringing in raw materials like iron ore from the Mesabi Range in Minnesota (via inexpensive water transportation on Lake Superior) and coal from Illinois (via railroads).
- Available land and labor: The city and its surrounding areas provided ample and affordable land for extensive industrial facilities. The burgeoning industry also attracted a large immigrant workforce from various countries, including Ireland, Scotland, Germany, Poland, and Serbia in the late 19th and early 20th centuries, followed by individuals from the Southern US and Mexico after World War I.
- Growing demand: Chicago's steel industry benefited from the increasing demand for steel in various sectors, including railroads, infrastructure projects like bridges and skyscrapers, and the manufacturing of goods like pipe, containers, and wire.

The industry saw significant expansion and consolidation in the late 19th century. In 1889, the Illinois Steel Company was formed through a merger of major

Chicago-area mills, including the North Chicago, South Works, Union, and Joliet plants. This company became the largest steel producer in the US and eventually merged with other steel and transportation companies to form the Federal Steel Company in 1898. Finally, in 1901, the Federal Steel Company was merged into U.S. Steel, which became the largest global corporation at the time.

The growth of the steel industry transformed the Calumet region, located south and east of Chicago, into a major industrial hub. This area, once characterized by wetlands, became home to numerous steel mills, including U.S. Steel's South Works and, in nearby Gary, Indiana, U.S. Steel's massive steel complex built in 1906. Other companies, such as Inland Steel, also established large mills in the Calumet district. In the hundred years following the first steel mill, the Chicago-Calumet district would produce more steel than anywhere else in the world.

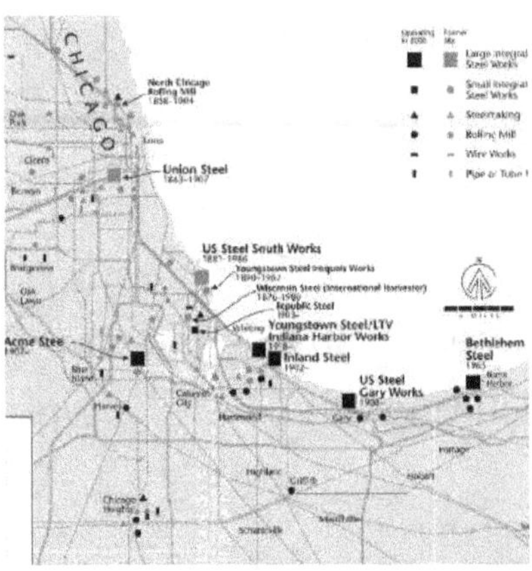

Industrial map of the steel industry in the Calumet region

Beginning in 1850, much of Chicago's heavy industry was pushed to the southeast side, which was isolated from the rest of the city. From there, the steel industry expanded across the border to Indiana, where mills were built along the shores of Lake Michigan. This collection of mills would supply the nation's need for steel for use in cars, skyscrapers, stoves, washers, bridges, housing, and countless other products.

The creation of US Steel resulted in the city of Gary, Indiana

Steel Unions at the Beginning

The earliest known union of steelworkers in Chicago was the Friendship Union Lodge, established in 1869. This union consisted of mill heaters, a highly skilled job responsible for maintaining raw steel at specific temperatures before it was shaped into products by intense pressure. This union became the Brotherhood of Iron and Steel Heaters, Rollers, and Roughers. Rollers and Roughers were also skilled workers who controlled the machinery, shaping red-hot steel into bars and billets. By 1874, the union had grown to about 750 members across 30 lodges nationwide. It did not include the lower-skilled crews at the rolling mills, leading to the creation of the Iron and Steel Roll Hands union at a north Chicago mill in 1870. Within a few years, this union expanded to 20 lodges and 500 members.

During the depression known as the Panic of 1873, the unions agreed to unite and formed the National Amalgamated Association of Iron and Steel Workers (hereinafter called the Amalgamated), with 3,800 members. During this time, there were many iron and steel companies, with intense competition and high profits from supplying the massive infrastructure being built as railroads expanded into the western U.S. Unions took advantage of this economy, with high pay rates, and their membership increased to 25,000 by 1890.

The industry entered a recession in the early 1890s, and some steel companies attempted to break the Amalgamated. In 1892, at Homestead, Pennsylvania, the Carnegie-owned mill lowered wages at the end of the contract. After battles with Pinkerton guards, the union lost the strike and lost members in other eastern mills.

Strikers battle the Pinkertons

Contemporary images of the battles at Homestead

The Amalgamated vs U.S. Steel

After its staggering defeat at Homestead, the Amalgamated Association still had a small hold in the industry for a few more years. The formation of U.S. Steel caused its next major setback in 1901. Andrew Carnegie, dismayed at the Homestead bloodshed, decided to get out of the business and devote his life to charity. J. P.

Morgan formed U.S. Steel on March 2, 1901, by financing the merger of Carnegie Steel Company with Elbert H. Gary's Federal Steel Company and William Henry Moore's National Steel Company for $492 million ($14.82 billion today). U.S. Steel became the largest steel producer and the largest corporation in the world. It was capitalized at $1.4 billion ($42.2 billion today), making it the world's first billion-dollar corporation. The new company controlled about two-thirds of the country's output of raw steel, four-fifths of its production of finished steel products, and employed 168,000 men.

The Amalgamated saw this massive organization as a crisis. They needed to organize the newly formed U.S. Steel plants before the corporation could stop their union drives. U.S. Steel management refused to recognize the union at its nonunion mills and refused to bargain with the AA at its unionized mills. A strike was called in August 1901, but U.S. Steel recruited strikebreakers by the thousands. The union appealed to Samuel Gompers, president of the American Federation of Labor, to support the strike. He refused. The strike was lost a month later, and the union accepted terms far worse than those it had initially been offered. In the end, U.S. Steel drove down wages so much that independent, nonunion mills had to cut wages just to stay competitive. By 1909, national membership in the AA had fallen to 6,300, and it would not be a force in the steel industry for another decade.

Aftermath of World War I

In the last half of the 1800s and into the 1900s, there was massive immigration from Europe into the United States. By 1900, a majority of workers in the steel industry were foreign-born. The AA maintained an aloof attitude towards immigrants and largely ignored local strikes at steel mills from 1910 to 1918.

During World War I, trade unionism made rapid strides in most of the industries of the country, but not in the steel industry. During the period of war, the Wilson administration gave its support to the principle of collective bargaining through the National War Labor Board. The Board said:

The right of workers to organize in trade unions and to bargain collectively through chosen representatives is recognized and affirmed. This right shall not be denied, abridged, or interfered with by the employers in any matter whatsoever.

War contracts contained a clause requiring submission of all disputes likely to interfere with production to the National War Labor Board. The clause did not appear in contracts for steel, and no steel industry case was submitted to the Board during the war period.

The 1919 Strike Wave

STRIKE CALLED

ALL UNIONS TO GO OUT

Seattle Union Record

SIXTY THOUSAND TO RESPOND TO CALL

NO CONSTRUCTIVE LEGISLATION YET

ANNOUNCEMENT OF STRIKE

35,000 SILK MILL WORKERS STRIKE

General strike in Seattle, 1919

In 1919, a total of four million American workers went out on strike – almost one quarter of the nation's industrial workforce. This was one of the largest waves of labor actions in American history. Among them were more than 350,000 steelworkers, 400,000 miners, as well as millions more in other sectors of the economy. These included Broadway actors and other theater workers; dress and waist makers in New York City, and elsewhere; the Boston police; and a general strike in Seattle. There were pitched battles and even bombs used. One exploded at the Washington, D.C., residence of Attorney General Mitchell Palmer. Palmer ordered raids that rounded up thousands of labor organizers and "anti-American subversives. "The post-war "red scare" hysteria was thrust into steel industry organizing.

The Strike in Chicago

In 1918, the Chicago stockyards were successfully organized under a plan developed by William Z. Foster, general organizer of the Brotherhood of Railway Carmen and a former leader of the Industrial Workers of the World (IWW).(Foster would become Chairman of the newly formed U.S. Communist Party in the 1920s.)Foster's idea was to have all the unions with members in the stockyards unite instead of trying to fight separately. This was successful, and collective bargaining was introduced into the packing industry.

William Z. Foster 1881 - 1961

Foster presented a similar plan for the steel industry to the 1918 convention of the American Federation of Labor (AFL).A committee of 25 national craft unions approved the plan to have a "hurricane drive" in all the steel centers of the U.S. at once. It was thought that this would force President Wilson to intervene in the war and thus impose a contract on the steel industry. This initial plan failed because the various unions moved too slowly and didn't contribute the funds needed for the organizing drive. Foster had estimated that $250,000 ($3.7 million today) was required for a national drive, but each union only contributed $100 ($1,500 today). The unions did contribute organizers, which Foster used as his base. The war ended in November 1918 before any organizing drives could take place.

Without funds for a truly national drive, Foster started close to home. He sent organizers to hold mass meetings in South Chicago, Gary, Indiana; Hammond, Indiana; and Joliet, Illinois. They received much support, but at the time, the Chicago area was not the heart of the steel industry; the Monongahela Valley in Pennsylvania was the key. Several months later, Foster sent organizers to that area. They were limited because authorities had banned most public meetings due to the deadly, massive influenza epidemic sweeping the country. Organizers held meetings in Youngstown, Cleveland, Buffalo, Johnstown, Wheeling, and Pittsburgh. They signed more than 100,000 steelworkers by early 1919. Alarmed, U.S. Steel tried to counter the union activity by granting a basic 8-hour day, meaning workers would get time-and-a-half for any hours beyond eight.

A union conference was held in Pittsburgh in late May 1919. Reports were submitted to the delegates detailing discharges for union membership, blacklisting, intimidation, and espionage. Judge Gary, U.S. Steel chairman, refused to meet with the delegates. A strike vote was called, and 98% were in favor of a walkout.

Blacksmith

BALLOT

IRON & STEEL WORKERS

The Union Committees are now seeking to get higher wages, shorter hours and better working conditions from the steel companies. Are you willing to back them up to the extent of stopping work should the companies refuse to concede these demands?

TAJNO GLASANJE

SZAVAZZON!

VOTAZIONE

HLASOVACI LISTOK

BALLOT

VOTE YES OR NO. Mark X in square indicating how you vote

Yes [X] No [ ]

National Committee for Organizing Iron and Steel Workers

WM. Z. FOSTER, Sec'y-Treas. 303 Magee Bldg., Pittsburgh, Pa.

Multi-language ballot is used to determine strike support.

Steelworkers had flocked to the organizing drive for several basic reasons. The primary cause was the excessive hours of work. Approximately one-half of the workers were subjected to a twelve-hour day. Of those, one-half worked a seven-day week. Only one quarter had a day of fewer than 10 hours, and the average workweek for all employees was 69 hours. Another reason was the "boss system". The mill organization was military in form, and the control was autocratic. Workers were not allowed to join unions. In addition, a frequent complaint was the failure of the steel companies to take precautions to prevent accidents. The steel industry ranked with the mining industry in fatal accidents.

The Great Steel Strike Begins

The negotiating committee spent several months trying to schedule a meeting with Judge Gary, Chairman of U.S. Steel. He finally sent a letter saying he did not believe in negotiating with unions but would deal with employees one-on-one. The committee reached out to President Wilson, but he was no more successful in getting Gary to meet with them.

On September 22, 1919, the strike began. Although only about 100,000 men had signed up, 275,000 responded to the strike call, and by the beginning of October, the number on strike had risen to some 365,000. At this point, the strike was 85-90 per cent effective. In Chicago, the *Chicago Tribune* reported 90,000 on strike, with all major plants closed except a few independents in Hammond, Indiana.

The demands were:

1.Right of collective bargaining.

2.Reinstatement of men discharged for union activity and paid for time lost.

3.The eight-hour day.

4.One day's rest in seven.

5.Abolition of 24-hour shifts.

6.Increase in wages sufficient to guarantee an American standard of living.

7.Standard scale of wages for all crafts, and classification of workers.

8.Double pay for overtime and Sunday, and holiday work.

9. Check-off system of collecting union dues and assessments.

10. The principle of seniority applies in maintaining, reducing, and increasing working forces.

11.Abolition of company unions.

12. Abolition of physical examination of applicants for employment.

Within a few days, U.S. Steel struck back. It announced it would reopen mills and resume operations and urged workers to return. The police said they would protect any workers coming back across picket lines.In Hammond, Indiana, a strike at the Standard Steel Car Company turned violent when four strikers were killed and dozens were wounded by police attempting to stop a strike rally.

The Gary Mills Arm

In Gary, groups of professionals and businessmen organized police auxiliaries to keep order and the plants in operation. One Chicago newspaper printed a front-page story:

Gary Arming For Battle On Strikers

Hundreds of Rifles Taken into Plants, Citizens Organize

Clerks at the Gary steel mills last night became armed guards with the arrival of rifles. Several cases were taken into the plant of the U.S. Steel Corporation, and 300 rifles were taken into the American Sheet and Tin Plant. Nearly 500 guards are on duty, and 400 clerks are aiding them.

Meanwhile, 600 Gary citizens, foreseeing the possibility of trouble, met in the Gary public library and formed a citizens' military police organization.

Most of those who remained at work were highly skilled, higher-paid Americans. Immigrant workers from southern and eastern Europe, who were more likely to support industrial rather than craft unionism, formed the backbone of the movement. Many of the strikers were men recently returned from the European battlefields. "We are all on the firing line once more," declared one striker, *"and we are going over the top as we did in 1918 over there. For we are determined to lick the steel barons of the country as we were to lick the German Kaiser."*

Strike leader speaking in Gary, Indiana.

FAIR WEATHER

THE LAKE COUNTY TIMES

BEST READ NEWSPAPER IN COUNTY

STEEL STRIKE GRIPS ENTIRE COUNTRY

END OF COMING CONFLICT HARD TO PREDICT

WALKOUT IN GARY IS WITHOUT DISORDER

DANGER IS LURKING IN STEEL STRIKE

FIGURES GIVEN OUT CONFLICTING

THOUSANDS ARE OUT IN IND. HARBOR

Steel Workers Strengthen Forces

DISORDER IS A MINUS QUANTITY

The steel companies were able to exploit Foster's known radicalism to paint the strike as an attempted revolution. (The strike was occurring at a time when not only was there a revolution in Russia, but there were civil insurrections in many of the post-war countries of Europe.)In addition, the United States had sent troops to protect assets in Russia during their ongoing civil war, so the issue of Bolsheviks and radical politics was on the public's mind. In Chicago, a large crowd of World War I veterans attacked and destroyed the IWW headquarters at 8749 S. Commercial, a short distance from the U.S. Steel mill in Chicago. The *Chicago Tribune* wrote, *"The decision to support the owners or the steelworkers means a choice between the American system and the Russian – individual liberty or dictatorship."*

Union racism was also a significant issue. The unions had racist policies that did not admit black workers. As a result, black workers gave the strike no support in the Pittsburgh area and little elsewhere. In the Chicago area, companies recruited large numbers of black workers from both black neighborhoods of Chicago and the Deep South. By late October, blacks were doing 75 percent of the work, and 95 percent had not worked in the mills before the strike. On October 7, martial law was declared in Gary, Indiana Harbor, and East Chicago. President Wilson ordered one thousand federal troops into the streets and they escorted strikebreakers through the picket lines.

National polls showed an increasing number of government officials and members of the public believed the strike was Communist inspired. The companies felt free to put down the strike by any means necessary. In Pennsylvania and Delaware, state police attacked strikers with clubs and dragged them out of their homes. In some areas, strikers were jailed and told they would be released if they went back to work. These confrontations led to 20 deaths nationally, including five in the Chicago district, but there were no significant battles such as occurred at Homestead.

Towards the end of November, the strike began to weaken seriously. By the middle of December, the number on strike had dropped to 110,000, and steel production had been restored to 60 percent of normal. There was a split within the union coalition. The Amalgamated ordered its men to return, citing the excuse that the skilled workers had contracts. The actions by the Amalgamated took 70,000 to 90,000 members from the organizing committee coalition, all recruited through the drive.

The Strike Ends

A majority of strikers had gone back to work by January, and the strike committee officially called off the strike on January 8, 1920. The strike was a failure for several reasons. The exclusion of blacks from AFL unions made it easy for blacks to be recruited as strikebreakers. Trying to organize the industry around two dozen craft unions led to each union looking out for its own interests. Workers in mass-production sectors such as steel, auto, and rubber would have to be organized into a single industry-wide union.

The U.S. Senate investigated the origins of the strike. The Senate concluded the wages were sufficient, but the hours worked were too long. The Senate report stated workers had a right to have representatives to present grievances. They accused radicals of promoting the strike.

The Senate recommended: *1) aid to workers to buy homes; 2) an 'Americanization' law to require education of foreign and native illiterates; 3) require the deporting of aliens who do not learn English in five years; 4) set up an agency similar to the War Labor Board; and 5) pass an anti-revolution law.*

Almost no union organizing in the steel industry occurred over the next 15 years. Advances in technology, such as the development of the wide-strip continuous sheet mill, made most skilled jobs in steelmaking obsolete. The Amalgamated Association, which only played a minor role in the 1919 steel strike, remained dormant until the creation of the Steel Workers Organizing Committee in 1936.

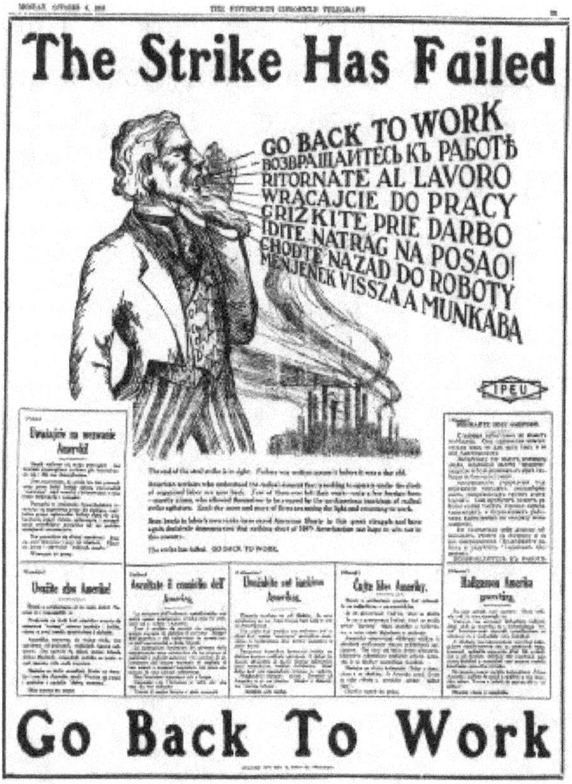

Steel companies placed ads in mill town newspapers urging workers to end the strike.

Each significant strike in 1919 ended in defeat for the workers. The active role of government intervention on the side of business proved too much for unions, which were still divided. But these strikes led to considerable advances in the 1930s. The public was educated about the poor working conditions of industrial workers, which led to pressure on the government to support change. In the steel industry, although the strike was lost, there was a victory in the work hours. The steel mills abandoned their seven-day 12-hour days. Although they did not adopt a standard workweek, it was a relief to many workers. Thus ended the great steel strike of 1919, a bitterly fought battle on the industrial front of U.S. history.

2 The Union Is Forged

The Dispute Over Organizing

Following the defeat of the 1919 strike, the Amalgamated Association tried to hold its membership gains. As a result of organizing activities during the strike, the Amalgamated had reached a peak membership of 32,000.

The 1920s were good for the steel industry but poor for organizing attempts. Steel production rose by 34 percent between 1920 and 1929.Other sectors that needed steel, such as the automobile, appliance, and container industries, also grew rapidly in the 1920s.A much more efficient method of rolling sheet steel was developed to meet the demand. The cost of electricity dropped, enabling the full use of the highly productive electric arc furnaces.

After the 1919 strike, most mills ended the 12-hour day in response to public and government criticism. Many companies, freed from wartime restrictions, moved to decrease wage rates. Some steel companies attempted to start Employee Representative Plans. These plans were company-created workplace organizations intended to keep traditional unions out.

During this time, there was a fundamental dispute in the labor movement over how to organize industrial workers. The craft-dominated AFL believed the most effective way to represent workers was to organize them by skill. They had a dismissive attitude towards "unskilled" mass production workers. They focused on skilled workers such as carpenters, machinists, and railroad engineers. They attempted to control what work their members performed through strict enforcement of jurisdictional work rules, control over apprenticeship programs, and the exclusion of less-skilled workers from membership. During the 1920s, most craft unions experienced significant growth. The building trades advanced from a membership of 78,950 in 1923 to 919,000 in 1929, the printing trades from 151,000 to 163,000, and the railway organizations, which were facing new competition from the automobile, only declined slightly from 597,000 to 565,000 members. Craft unions, with their conservative outlook on both internal and general matters, came to dominate the AFL Executive Council and general policy.

The proponents of industrial unionism generally believed that craft distinctions were appropriate in industries where craft unions had flourished, such as construction or printing, but unworkable in sectors such as steel or auto production. In their view, dividing workers in a single plant into multiple crafts, each represented by a separate organization with its own agenda, would weaken workers' bargaining power and leave the majority, who had few traditional craft skills, completely unrepresented. Although the AFL had always included several industrial unions, such as the United Mine Workers, the hardline craft unionists held a strong sway over the federation. It used its power to shut down any drive towards industrial organizing. In steel, the AFL set up organizing committees in Gary, South Chicago, Joliet, and nearby areas.

The leadership of the Amalgamated Association was accused by the rank and file of acting in their own personal interest. The leaders seemed to be content to maintain the status quo, as it provided them with a comfortable living while ignoring organizing opportunities. An insurgency developed within the Amalgamated in the 1920s, drawing on lessons from the 1919 strike about industrial unionism.

Company Unions Are Created

During this period, some mills decided to create what were called Employee Representation Plans (ERPs).At Wisconsin Steel in South Chicago, owned by International Harvester, a "works council" was established before the 1919 strike. The ERP attempted to discourage workers from joining the strike and helped screen out unionists when the company rehired workers after the strike was defeated. In return, the company allowed some concessions and a slight wage increase. Inland Steel, in East Chicago, also promoted an ERP for the same purposes. In addition, some mills adopted pension and insurance plans to forestall unionism. These pension plans were not protected by law and could be revoked at the company's discretion. Union activity could be grounds for denying pension rights.

The Depression Hits

By August 1932, employment in the steel industry had dropped by 50 percent. By the following year, only 40,000 workers were employed in Chicago-area steel mills, compared to the 100,000 employed during the 1919 steel strike. Only two percent of those employed in 1933 were covered by union agreements.

The incoming Roosevelt administration passed the National Industrial Recovery Act, which spurred union organization in the steel industry, among others. Section 7(a) of the NRA code recognized the right of workers to organize and bargain collectively. Under pressure, the Amalgamated sent two organizers to Chicago. Initial results were so promising that within a few months, 106 organizers were in the field nationally. In Chicago, advertisements were placed in newspapers, and time was purchased on the radio. Importantly, the Amalgamated remembered a lesson from the 1919 strike and did not draw a color line when recruiting.

The steel companies did not let this activity go unnoticed. They actively attempted to counter union organizing by increasing the use of ERPs. In the year before the NRA was passed, only 20 percent of workers were covered by employee representative plans. This figure increased to 94 percent by the end of 1934.Chicago union members put pressure on the national Amalgamated to call a strike day, but intervention by the Roosevelt administration forestalled any strike activity.

John L. Lewis Comes to the Scene

John L. Lewis 1880 - 1969

In the middle of this dispute came John L. Lewis. Lewis went to work in the mines in southern Illinois at age 16 and was later elected president of his United Mine Workers local. He lobbied the Illinois legislature on behalf of workers' compensation and mine safety legislation.

Samuel Gompers, AFL president, recognized his work and hired him as a national field representative. In 1920, he became president of the United Mine Workers (UMW).At the beginning of the 1920s, Lewis leveraged the nation's dependence on coal to maintain union membership despite periodic economic downturns in the industry. The unionized mines faced intense competition from nonunion operators, including the 'captive mines' the steel companies owned and operated, which provided coke and coal for steel production. When the Great Depression hit in 1929, there was a significant drop in mine union membership. Lewis, along with some other labor leaders, came to the understanding that their own unions could not survive while the great majority of workers in basic industry remained nonunion. So long as the steel industry remained nonunion, pressure could be put on the captive mines to stay nonunion. Throughout the country, coal operators were using the competitive advantage of the captive mines to attack the UMW. Lewis and industrial union leaders started to press the AFL to change its organizing policies.

The AFL authorized organizing drives in the automobile, rubber, and steel industries at its 1934 convention, but provided little financial support or effective leadership to those unions. The AFL's timidity made it less credible among the workers it supposedly sought to organize. This was important in industries such as steel and rubber, where workers organized at significant personal risk.

Lewis Throws a Punch

The dispute came to a head at the AFL's convention in 1935.Lewis demanded that the convention make good on their promises to organize and charter industrial unions.

The convention defeated all of his proposals. William Hutcheson, the President of the United Carpenters, made a mocking comment about a rubber worker who was delivering an organizing report. Lewis and Hutcheson exchanged a few words, and Lewis leaped over a row of chairs and knocked Hutcheson to the ground with a right to the nose. Lewis then relit his cigar and returned to the rostrum. The blow symbolized the breach between the craft and industrial unions and helped cement Lewis's image in the public eye as someone willing to fight for the workers' right to organize.

Shortly afterward, Lewis called a meeting of eight industrial unions and, on November 9, 1935, created the Committee for Industrial Organization (CIO).The AFL leadership treated the CIO as an enemy from the outset, refusing to deal with it and demanding its dissolution. The AFL's opposition to the CIO only increased the stature of the CIO and Lewis in the eyes of industrial workers who wanted to organize and had been dissatisfied with the AFL's ineffective performance.

Making full use of his notoriety, Lewis committed UMW funds to support organizing drives in the rubber, auto, and steel industries. Without his support and without Lewis's involvement, it is doubtful whether these campaigns would have succeeded. Lewis assigned his own staff to assist each drive, remained in constant communication with them, and personally negotiated agreements with General Motors and U.S. Steel.

The Flint Sit Down Strike

The Flint sit-down strike lasted 44 days before victory

The CIO's initial strategy was to focus its efforts on the steel industry and use success there to expand into other industries. The workers in the auto industry would not wait. With New Deal Democrats in key positions of power, the newly hired organizers employed by the CIO targeted an auto assembly plant in Flint, Michigan, in early January 1937, for a sit-down strike that would serve as an ideal starting point and signal what was to come. The auto factory was chosen because General Motors owned it and was a critical link in the company's network of factories. Success would bring much of General Motors' production to a halt. Moreover, a victory over the third-largest corporation in the country was likely to bring hope to industrial workers everywhere. Its profits had rebounded in 1935 and 1936, leading to $10 million ($185 million today) in salaries and bonuses for 350 officers and directors in 1936, while its workers averaged $900 ($16,650 today) a year, well below the $1,600 ($29,600 today) that was considered to be the minimum necessary for a family of four. Led in good part by Communist and Socialist factions in the fledgling United Auto Workers, the sit-downers held the factory for six weeks despite attacks by police, legal threats from local authorities, and demands by the owners that the liberal governor put an end to this illegal takeover of private property. However, neither the governor nor President Roosevelt would accede to the corporation's demands, forcing its leaders to negotiate with the union and thereby providing a significant triumph for the CIO.

The SWOC Forms

In the steel industry, the CIO initially attempted to work within the existing Amalgamated Association. If they could get the AA to change its mind about organizing along industrial lines, the AFL could do nothing to stop an organizing drive. The CIO offered $500,000 ($9.2 million today) for an organizing drive in steel, and the AA accepted. The AA became a unit of the newly formed Steel Workers Organizing Committee (SWOC) on June 7, 1936.This led the AFL to declare that the CIO was engaging in "dual unionism" and to suspend the ten CIO unions. Philip Murray, a UMW official, was appointed director of the SWOC and given 35 organizers to run the campaign. David McDonald was appointed Secretary-

Treasurer. Van Bittner was placed in charge of the Chicago region.

Unlike the UAW's success against GM at Flint, the organizing campaign in the steel industry was a top-down affair. Lewis, who had a particular interest in organizing the steel industry because of its essential role in the coal industry where UMW members worked, dispatched two hundred organizers to sign up members. The SWOC policy was to enroll all members of a plant or mill into the same local, regardless of craft or department. Many of them were Lewis's past political opponents or radicals drawn from the Communist-led unions that had attempted to organize the industry earlier in the 1930s.Lewis was not concerned with his organizers' political beliefs, so long as he controlled the organization. He remarked, when asked about "reds" on the SWOC staff, *"Who gets the bird? The hunter or the dog?"*

The SWOC kicked off the organizing campaign with spirited rallies at McKeesport and Homestead and a stirring nationwide radio address by Lewis. With the $500,000 funding from the Miners' union, the SWOC staffed a new headquarters in Pittsburgh with paid professionals and soon launched a weekly newspaper, *Steel Labor*.

During the summer of 1936, hundreds of organizers fanned out to the mill towns. They made it easy to sign up, waiving the $3 ($55 in today's dollars) initiation fee and deferring the $1 monthly dues. In six months, SWOC collected 125,000 membership cards, about a quarter of the entire workforce.

Lewis and U.S. Steel Have Lunch

The big breakthrough came in January 1937.Lewis was lunching at the Mayflower Hotel in Washington, D.C. It happened that the chairman of U.S. Steel, Myron Taylor, was also having lunch there. The two men chatted informally and agreed to meet the next day. It was a stunning moment; the head of the Mine Workers union talking with the head of the country's most powerful antiunion corporation. Over the next few weeks, Lewis and Taylor met in secret a dozen times, usually at Taylor's townhouse in New York City.(The meetings were so secret that other top union and company officials did not know of them.)

Confronted with growing union organizational muscle and with war preparation in Europe creating a heavy demand for armor plate, the corporation sought labor peace and stability. In addition, Taylor wanted to avoid the chaos and business losses GM had faced while fighting the UAW in Flint. Also, New Deal Democrats controlled Pennsylvania, where the company had many of its mills. Furthermore, SWOC was winning over many members of the company-sponsored employee representation plan. In effect, union organizers were building an industrial union at U.S. Steel and elsewhere, through the employee representation plans

Lewis and the SWOC achieved stunning success when on March 2, 1937 U.S. Steel announced that it had agreed to a ten percent wage hike to $5 ($93 today) a day in the northern mills; an eight-hour day and forty-hour week, with overtime; seniority protection; a basic grievance procedure; and most important, full recognition of the SWOC as a bargaining agent for its members.[**See Appendix B-2 for the whole agreement.**] The agreement was shocking to other steel companies and to anyone who remembered the union-busting tactics of the Carnegie-Frick days. Two weeks after the public announcement, the two sides met in U.S. Steel's massive conference room to sign the formal papers. There, someone noticed a black space among the portraits of corporation executives. *"Whose picture was there?"* he asked. *"Old H.C. Frick,"* went the reply. *"They took him out. Didn't think he could stand it."*

The agreement saved Lewis from expending resources on what could have been a very long and arduous battle, kept the many Communist organizers from rising to essential positions in what was basically a top-down union, and provided a visible symbolic victory because U.S. Steel was the largest industrial company in the United States.

SWOC Turns to Little Steel

While mill organizing was going on, SWOC scored a victory in the most critical labor relations court case of the modern era. During SWOC's attempt to organize Jones & Laughlin Steel in 1936, the company summarily fired hundreds of union supporters. SWOC filed an unfair labor practice against the company and won. Jones & Laughlin appealed to the court, alleging that the National Labor Relations Act was unconstitutional. But in *National Labor Relations Board v. Jones & Laughlin Steel Corporation,* 301 U.S. 1 (1937), the U.S. Supreme Court upheld the Act's constitutionality.

By the middle of 1937, half a million steelworkers had joined the union in 750 local lodges. Including U.S. Steel, 125 companies had signed union contracts employing 310,000 workers. But the major independents, known as Little Steel, still held out. These companies – American Rolling Mill, Bethlehem, Inland, National, Republic, and Youngstown Sheet and Tube – were "little" only in comparison to U.S. Steel. In reality, they were major corporations with abundant resources, and their leaders were fiercely anti-union. These companies employed 186,000 workers and accounted for 40% of steel production. The contract settlement at U.S. Steel only strengthened their determination to resist any further encroachment on the industry's open-shop tradition. Unlike U.S. Steel, these companies were willing to use violence, espionage, and large numbers of strikebreakers to crush the union. Tom Girdler, head of Republic Steel, was appointed by the other Little Steel companies to lead the fight against the union. He remarked, *"Regardless of whether every man in the Republic joins the Union, we are not going to recognize it. We are not going to sign any contract. We will shut the mills down and board them up before we sign with the CIO .If I have to spend the rest of my life dealing with John L. Lewis, I would rather raise apples and potatoes."*[**See Appendix B-1 for an example of Republic Steel's opposition**]

The Strike Begins

Murray and the SWOC tried to bargain with the Little Steel companies for several months after the U.S. Steel contract was signed. Finally, the union decided it must strike. The walkout began on May 26, 1937, eventually involving 90,000 steelworkers in seven states. The companies had been preparing for battle for several months. After the strike, a U.S. Senate investigation found the Chicago Republic steel mill had purchased 550 revolvers, 65 rifles, 245 shotguns, 143 gas guns, 4,000 tear gas projectiles, 2,700 gas grenades, and a large number of nightsticks. This willingness by Republic Steel to use violence directly led to the most violent incident, which occurred in the formation of the Steelworkers Union.

The Chicago Memorial Day Massacre

Initially, about 500 men walked out of the Chicago Republic plant on May 26th.Several hundred remained working. The company set up dormitories for them inside the unfinished wire mill. The strikers attempted to set up a picket line at the gate but were met by 100 Chicago police officers. They attacked the picket line, using clubs, and arrested 23.Two days later, another attempt was made to form a picket line, but it was attacked again. This resulted in 16 men being hospitalized. The union and others appealed to Mayor Kelly. The mayor said that picketing was legal and the strikers could have as many as they wanted. The Police Commissioner agreed.

Taking the word of these city officials, the strikers called a meeting on Sunday, Memorial Day, May 30th, at their headquarters, a tavern called Sam's Place, three blocks from the mill gate. Unknown to the SWOC, the police had received false information that the strikers would attempt to invade the plant on Sunday and drive out non-union workers. In response, the police ordered 265 officers to the mill. When the meeting began Sunday afternoon, 1,500 were present. Not only were there strikers, but family members and sympathizers from other mills. As the speeches ended, someone from the crowd suggested a march to the main gate to establish a picket line. The crowd chanted, *"CIO! CIO!"* as they moved down the dirt road to the mill gate. Many of the marchers carried picket signs denouncing Republic Steel's labor policies or proclaiming the right to picket. The main body of police moved two blocks towards the marchers. Another group of police moved to prevent the marchers from making an end run around the line to the mill gate entrance.

March leaders asked permission to go to the gate and establish a picket line. The police refused the request and ordered them to disperse. The crowd was chanting pro-union slogans, and many were shouting at the police. Paramount Newsreel Films had a cameraman recording the events, but he was changing the lens when the actual violence began. His film is available online. There were many still pictures of the event. Some of the marchers, frustrated by the police, started throwing stones or using slingshots. One officer fired a warning shot in the air, and others drew their weapons. The missiles from some in the crowd continued, and tear gas canisters were launched by police in response. Police in the rear began to fire in the air, and then the police in the front fired their weapons at the crowd. The marchers fell back and fled in confusion and horror. People stumbled on top of one another as the police attack continued. In 15 seconds, about 180 shots were fired by the police. Although newspapers reported someone in the crowd had fired at least one shot, there was never any hard evidence.

The police moved forward using their batons on marchers who had fallen or were wounded. Some police dragged marchers, injured or not, and dumped them into patrol wagons. The crowd retreated to Sam's Place, where wounded and injured were treated by doctors. When the bodies were counted, four had been fatally shot, with six more to die in the next few days. Another 30 were wounded, and dozens more were hospitalized. Of the four dozen gunshot wounds, only four were frontal, and most were back wounds. None of the police had been badly injured. The most serious was a broken arm, and 30 others had cuts and bruises.

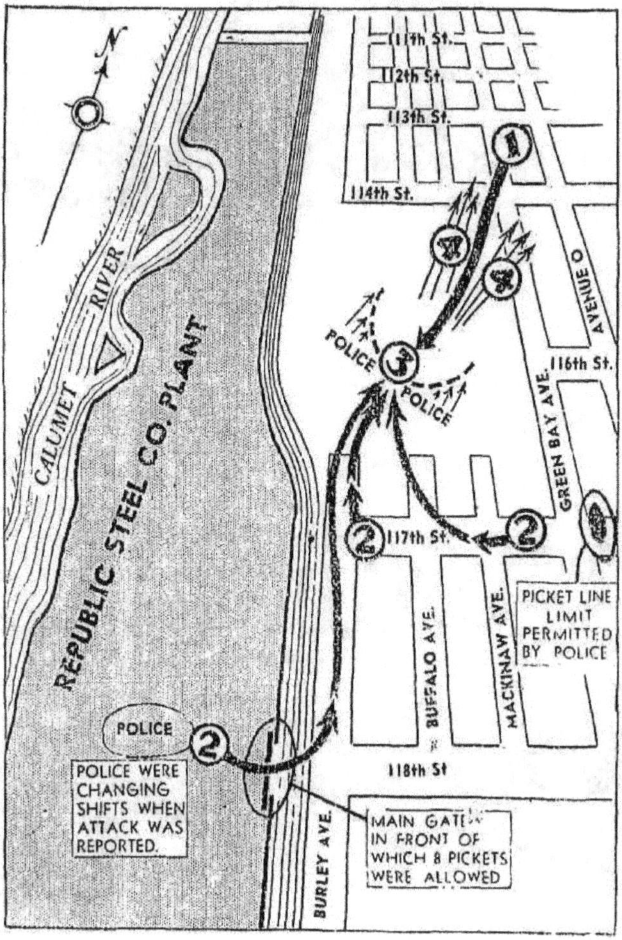

Map showing the route of marchers and police movements.

Sam's Place, which was a bar that served as strike headquarters.
(11317 Green Bay Avenue, Chicago)

Marchers reach the police line

The moment the shots start.

Police attack marchers as they try to flee.

Police continuing to club strikers and supporters.

Police load a victim into a vehicle

People demanding answers to the violence from Mayor Kelly.

Poster announcing funeral service for the dead men.

This cartoon by the Tribune represents the city's media attitude towards the strikers

Sign commemorating the Memorial Day Massacre near the site.

The following strikers and supporters died: **Hilding Anderson**, 29, blood poisoning from a wound; **Alfred Causey**, 43, four bullet wounds; **Leo Francisco**, 17, a back wound; **Earl Handley**, 37, an untreated hemorrhage; **Otis Jones**, 33, a bullet in the back; **Sam Popovich**, 50, a broken skull; **Kenneth Reed**, 23, bled out in a patrol wagon; **Joseph Rothmund**, 48, back wound; **Anthony Tagliori**, 26, bullet in back; and **Lee Tisdale**, 50, blood poisoning from a bullet wound. In the following days, two strikers were killed at the Republic mill in Youngstown, Ohio, and four were killed at the Republic plant in Massillon, Ohio.

A United States Senate investigation of the violence questioned the police's actions in interfering with the picketing. It condemned the use of firearms. The Paramount film was shown in the Senate and around the country. Ironically, the city's Film Censorship Board would not allow the film to be shown in Chicago.

The Strike Ends

The violence and anti-union feelings took their toll, and the strike was called off in September 1937. Republic refused to take back many of the union organizers. SWOC filed a complaint with the National Labor Relations Board (NLRB).A long court battle followed. Finally, in August 1942, the NLRB ordered Republic to negotiate a contract with the union. The company complied, fearing loss of government World War II contracts. As part of the settlement, Republic Steel agreed to reinstate all active strikers to their former jobs with back pay of nearly $500,000 ($7.9 million today). The steel company also paid $350,000 ($5.5 million today) in damages to the injured and the families of the dead. No police were ever prosecuted. During this time, all of the Little Steel companies signed similar contracts, and the steel industry was at long last unionized.

Philip Murray decided it was time to transform the SWOC into a complete international union. On May 22, 1942, in Cleveland, 1,700 delegates gave birth to the United Steelworkers of America (USW).In less than six years, the SWOC had organized the vast majority of the nation's steelworkers into one large industrial union, breaking an employer stranglehold that had existed since the 1890s. Murray was elected as its first President, and David McDonald was elected as its first Secretary-Treasurer. By this time, Lewis had broken with Roosevelt in the 1940 election campaign and resigned from CIO leadership when Roosevelt was re-elected. Murray was chosen to head the CIO. Lewis remained as head of the Mine Workers.

3 Fighting to Preserve Gains

Post-War Strife

The Great Depression was only ended by the economic buildup to the Second World War. Millions of men went into the military, reducing the unemployment rate. Military-related orders pumped up the economy. During the war, unions and companies were placed under wage and price freezes for the duration of the conflict. When peace came in late 1945, many people feared a return of the Depression. Inflation jumped, and the massive strikes and labor disorder of 1945-46 did little to assuage those fears.

This era saw a massive influx of workers into the labor force. Over 10 million soldiers were discharged from the military between 1945 and 1947. At the same time, many millions of union members had worked in war industries during World War II. Their unions had postponed any significant demands in the name of national unity. Once Japan surrendered, these demands resurfaced and led to the most extensive series of labor actions in American history. Over five million workers went on strike during the first year after World War II.

The first big strike occurred among the oil workers, less than a month after Japan's surrender. Hours remained at their elevated wartime levels, without pay increases, and 43,000 workers went on strike. In October, Harry Truman ordered the Navy to seize many of the refineries and for the workers to return. This episode was just a footnote compared to what followed. In November, the United Auto Workers struck against General Motors for 113 days. Walter Reuther led 320,000 workers and won a 17.5% pay increase.

By 1946, strikes proliferated to the point that a national crisis was at hand. The average worker was caught in a squeeze between rising living costs and the wartime wage freeze, which remained in effect. Electrical workers, meatpackers, lumbermen, and teamsters all had their labor actions. Rochester and Pittsburgh saw general strikes. In December 1946, Oakland, California, witnessed a general strike in which over 100,000 people participated. In total, 25 percent of union members went out on strike in 1946. In addition to the GM strike, among the most significant actions were strikes by 200,000 electrical workers, 260,000 meat packers, and 750,000 steelworkers. The USW filed a petition with the National Labor Relations Board for a strike vote on wages. Steelworkers voted by a five-to-one margin to strike. In January 1946, the steelworkers went on strike for three weeks. When the USW received an offer of an 18.5 cents per hour ($2.40 in 2025 dollars) wage increase, Murray accepted the offer and ended the USW strike on February 15, 1946.

The most famous incidents, however, occurred in early 1946. First, Harry Truman faced off with the United Mine Workers (UMW) and, shortly thereafter, with the nation's railroad workers. The UMW was led by John L. Lewis, a man who'd worked in the mines as a teenager and thereafter dedicated his life to the mineworkers. In March 1946, he led 350,000 of them into a coal strike. Shortly thereafter, the two largest railroad unions also went on strike. While Truman generally supported labor, he also feared an end to the postwar recovery and a crippling of European aid and his political prospects. He ordered the federal government to seize the affected coal mines until a settlement was reached, and threatened to draft striking rail workers into the U.S. Army.

Many of the strikes, however, did lead to some concessions. Numerous unions won wage increases, and real wages throughout the U.S. generally rose in the years after World War II. So too did prices. The official inflation rate was 8% in 1946, 14% in 1947, and 8% again in 1948. This was a stressful development for those who, for whatever reason, did not see their incomes increase accordingly.

The USWA vs. UAW on Labor's Role

Under the leadership of Philip Murray, the United Steelworkers had gone out on strike on January 21, 1946, to secure higher wages. Unlike UAW President Reuther, however, Murray did not view collective bargaining as a vehicle for achieving broader social or economic gains for America as a whole. Just days after the steel strike settlement, the steel industry received permission from the Office of Price Administration—a federal agency set up during World War II to set prices and stop wartime inflation—to increase the price of steel by more than five dollars a ton. The price increase seemed to justify Reuther's argument that corporations would pass the wage costs to consumers and thereby fuel inflation. Reuther was disillusioned by Murray's refusal to speak out against the steel industry's action. Reuther realized that the USW's settlement left the UAW in a vulnerable bargaining position, as its strike had lasted almost three months by the time the USW settled.

This was the beginning of the political and social split between the nation's two largest industrial unions. The GM and steel industry strikes highlighted the crucial question for the postwar labor movement: should unions seek a voice in management, or should they be limited to bargaining over wages and benefits during contract talks? Reuther, who viewed the labor movement as a vehicle for social and economic change, fell into the first category. Murray, who held a bread-and-butter vision of unionism, was skeptical of such far-reaching plans. In the end, Murray's vision would predominate in postwar collective bargaining.

The strikes did not win support from the majority of Americans. In the 1946 Congressional Elections, the Republican Party gained 55 seats and control of the House for the first time since 1930. Conservative sentiment in the

U.S. was galvanized by opposition to the strikes, while liberals were divided over Truman's actions.

The Taft-Hartley Act

The Republicans used their majority to pass the Taft-Hartley Act over Truman's veto. This law, formally known as the Labor–Management Relations Act of 1947, amends much of the pro-union Wagner Act of 1935. A variety of factors, including the fear of Communist infiltration of labor unions, the tremendous growth in both union membership and power, and a series of large-scale strikes, contributed to an anti-union climate in the United States after World War II. The law received significant support from congressional Democrats, many of whom joined with their Republican colleagues in voting to override Truman's veto. The act continued to generate opposition after Truman left office, but it remains in effect.

The Taft–Hartley Act amended the 1935 National Labor Relations Act (NLRA), prohibiting unions from engaging in several "unfair labor practices." Among the practices prohibited by the act are jurisdictional strikes, wildcat strikes, solidarity or political strikes, secondary boycotts, secondary and mass picketing, closed shops, and monetary donations by unions to federal political campaigns. The NLRA also allowed states to pass right-to-work laws banning union shops. Enacted during the early stages of the Cold War, the law required union officers to sign non-communist affidavits with the government.

Union leaders in the CIO vigorously campaigned for Truman in the 1948 election based upon a (never fulfilled) promise to repeal Taft-Hartley. Truman won, but despite his opposition to the law, he relied upon it in twelve instances during his presidency.

Rally against the Taft-Hartley Act.

Truman Seizes the Steel Industry

The Steelworkers' first big test after World War II came as the Korean War raged. With contracts expiring the union indicated in September, 1951, that they would seek an industry-wide rather than company-by-company approach to the upcoming negotiations. Due to the war, the government had formed the Wage Stabilization Board (WSB) to control wages and inflation. Talks with U.S. Steel opened in November. Benjamin Fairless, president of U.S. Steel, said the steel industry as a group had no intention of reaching a collective bargaining agreement with the union. Further, he said workers were overpaid by at least 30 percent. The union asked for a substantial wage increase, overtime pay for weekend work, the union shop, and eight days of vacation a year. The companies refused to discuss economic issues on the grounds it was up to the WSB.

Negotiations continued without effect, and in January, hearings began before the WSB. The steel companies started a massive public relations campaign. Designed to emphasize the patriotism of the steel companies during wartime, the campaign was carried out in newspapers and on radio and television stations nationwide. The campaign attacked not only the union but also the WSB and the Truman administration. The public relations campaign asserted *"runaway inflation"* would occur if steelworkers' pay rose even minimally. A pay increase, it was said, would ruin the economy of the Deep South, *"hamper the country's defense against atomic attack, undermine our foreign economic policy, and introduce totalitarianism.* "They also charged that union proposals would create such inefficiency that workers would be driven to *"radicalism and communism"* in sheer frustration.

As time went on with no real movement in the negotiations, President Truman began to consider his options, and a seizure of the nation's steel mills seemed the most likely course. Truman was told that ammunition supplies in Korea were low, and that even a 10-day strike would endanger the war effort. Atomic weapons projects would be curtailed, 1,500 miles of highway would not be built, and U.S. commitments under the Mutual Defense Assistance Act could not be met, which might encourage Soviet aggression. Truman ruled out using the Taft–Hartley Act, believing it was unfair and unlikely to ensure steel production. Most of Truman's advisors favored the seizure of the steel mills under the inherent powers of the president as commander-in-chief.

The steel talks collapsed on April 4th, and the union notified the steel manufacturers that day that it planned to call a nationwide strike, which would begin at 12:01 a.m. on April 9th.

That evening, President Truman announced in a national television and radio address that he had issued Executive Order 10340 and he was ordering Secretary of Commerce Charles W. Sawyer to seize the nation's steel mills to ensure the continued production of steel. Truman attacked the steel companies' price demands, explained why he was not using the other legal options open to him, and called on the employers and union to meet in Washington the following day to negotiate a new collective bargaining agreement. The union immediately called off its strike, even though Sawyer announced he had no intention of giving them a wage increase.

The press was almost unanimous in its condemnation of the steel mill seizure. The *New York Daily News* headline was typical: **"Truman Does a Hitler".** Congress, too, reacted negatively. There were calls for Truman's impeachment, and several bills were introduced to strip the WSB of its powers, to permit the government to end the strike, and to withdraw congressional approval of the expenditure of funds to operate the steel plants. The steel companies also condemned the action. Clarence B. Randall, president of Inland Steel, gave a nationally broadcast speech on April 9th, attacking Truman and the Steelworkers. The employers' public relations group, "Steel Companies in the Wage Case", undertook an ambitious advertising campaign against the Truman administration. Full-page advertisements in major metropolitan newspapers appeared the next day, excoriating the seizure. Within a week, tens of thousands of pamphlets and fact sheets supporting the steel manufacturers' position had been produced.

Cartoon attacking Truman for seizing the steel mills.

The case quickly moved through the courts, and the Supreme Court heard the case on May 12th. As they waited for a decision, the steel companies continued their campaign to persuade the public. *"Hitler and Mussolini did the same thing in Germany and Italy as Truman has done in the United States,"* declared the president of Weirton Steel.

On June 2, 1952, in a 6-3 ruling, the Supreme Court declared in Youngstown Sheet & Tube Co. v. Sawyer, 343 U.S. 579 (1952) that the president lacked the authority to seize the steel mills. Writing for the majority, Justice Black held the president had no authority under the Constitution to seize private property on the grounds of national security. Since Congress had not otherwise authorized the president to seize the steel mills, the president could not do so. This case is one of the most famous in interpreting presidential power and is taught in law schools today.

The Strike Begins

The mills were returned to their owners immediately, and the union started the strike a few hours later. The economic impact of the strike began to be felt immediately. Layoffs in several steel-dependent industries occurred just two days after the strike began. National defense mobilization authorities began denying manufacturers of consumer goods steel four days after the strike started, and banned the export of steel on June 10th.By June 17th, defense plants producing the M47 Patton tank, the M41 Walker Bulldog tank, trucks, bazooka rockets, and mortar shells had all shut down or were running half- or quarter-shifts. By June 21st, steel inventories were almost depleted, forcing manufacturing shutdowns in the auto industry. As the Independence Day holiday neared, most inventories of steel were gone, even from defense stockpiles.

Truman's advisors told him to invoke the Taft-Hartley Act and send the union back to work, but Truman felt the law would do little to end the strike. President Murray of the Steelworkers worried that the strike's impact on national defense would turn public opinion against it. On June 19th, a limited number of union members agreed to return to work to finish and deliver steel for specific critical defense needs.

The Strike Ends

Several events weakened employers' bargaining position:

First, small steelmakers once more began breaking ranks. The union began negotiating contracts with small, weaker steel producers. Several other agreements seemed near, leading the larger companies to fear that they were losing the battle for employer sentiment.

Second, the Office of Price Stabilization agreed to a new, higher price increase for steel tonnage. The new offer to steel mills was for $5.60 a ton. Putnam offered the steelmakers the latest price on July 15th, but it was conditional on a swift resolution to the strike. The price increase worsened the position of the six largest employers compared to the smaller manufacturers.

Third, President Truman let it be known that he was considering nationalizing the steel mills under Section 18 of the Selective Service Act. Truman decided to invoke Section 18 in mid-June. To overcome the legal objections to the Act's use raised in early April, the government began placing direct steel orders on June 12th. On July 19th, *The New York Times* reported that Truman was expected to invoke Section 18 within a week. The threat of another government takeover of the steel mills—this time on solid legal ground, with adequate preparation by the government, and with the appearance of even-handedness (steelworkers would be drafted and ordered to work in the mills)—brought the manufacturers to the bargaining table again.

By this time, the strike had severely affected the nation. Half a million workers were laid off as companies lacked steel to keep plants running. The number of railroad cars loaded in the week ending July 7, 1952, was the lowest since records had been kept, and many railroads began to suffer financial difficulty. California growers lost $200 million because there wasn't enough tin to make tin cans for their crops. On July 22, the United States Army shut down its largest shell-making plant due to a lack of steel.

The shutdown of the Army facility proved to be the last straw for Truman. On the evening of July 23rd, Truman ordered the steelmakers and the union to meet in the White House the following day and settle the strike. At 10:00 a.m. on July 24th, Murray and Fairless were ushered into the Oval Office. Truman informed the two men of top-secret statistics that showed the U.S. war effort in Korea was being crippled. The President then told Fairless, "You can settle this thing, Ben, and you've got to settle it. I want it settled by tomorrow morning, or I will have some things to say that you won't like to hear, and I will have to do some things you won't like." Truman then turned to Murray and said, *"Phil, you've got to settle this thing, too. Now go in there in the Cabinet room, and I want you to come out with a settlement."* The two men adjourned to the Cabinet Room. At 4:45 p.m., Fairless and Murray told the President that they had reached an agreement.

Outcome

The strike was settled on essentially the same terms offered to the employers at the start of the strike. Workers received a 16-cent-an-hour wage increase ($1.55 in 2025 dollars), and a 6-cent-an-hour rise in fringe benefits. The wage and benefit package was a penny below the WSB's recommendation but markedly higher than anything the employers had publicly offered. The workers also won a version of the union shop: New employees were required to join the union, but could resign between the 15th and 30th day of employment (which few were expected to do).

The strike led to significant economic costs. The loss of economic output was estimated at $4 billion (equivalent to approximately $37,739,348,371 in 2025 dollars), 1.5

million people were pushed into unemployment before full steel production resumed, and the Federal Reserve estimated that industrial output dropped to 1949 levels. More than 19 million tons of steel were lost — roughly 90 percent of total steel production — for two months. Nearly four-fifths of the nation's small defense contractors were forced to close. Officials observed that several thousand small- and medium-sized businesses would close or operate on a part-time basis until steel production resumed (it would take three weeks for furnaces to be cleaned, relit, and brought back into production, and four weeks for steel to reach manufacturers).

The strike led Congress to strip the Wage Stabilization Board of its authority to resolve labor disputes. President Truman struggled to reconstitute the Board in his remaining five months in office. The Board never resumed its whole operation and was abolished by President Eisenhower in March 1953.

Murray and the union leaders considered the strike a significant win. The union had avoided the imposition of a Taft–Hartley injunction, Truman had gone to tremendous lengths to protect the union, and the union shop was won for the first time in the steel industry.

Murray Dies, McDonald Takes Over

Philip Murray died soon after the 1952 strike, and USW Secretary-Treasurer David McDonald was named

President by the International Executive Board. In negotiations, McDonald began to emphasize increasing fringe benefits. In 1948, the National Labor Relations Board ruled that non-economic items such as health benefits were subject to collective bargaining. Companies had no choice but to negotiate with unions, and the Steelworkers, along with other unions, fought hard to get them. McDonald focused negotiations on benefits such as unemployment compensation supplements, pensions, health insurance, tuition reimbursement, and more. McDonald transformed the steel industry contract from a basic wage-and-hour document into the framework that exists today.

Industry-Wide Bargaining

McDonald's first significant move was to push for industry-wide bargaining in the steel industry. Since the formation of the SWOC, the union had bargained first with U.S. Steel, then used that agreement as a pattern for the rest of the industry. The same thing happened with steel prices, which were set by U.S. Steel and then followed by its competitors. Bargaining with just U.S. Steel was inefficient because negotiators had to take the basic economic settlement and adjust it to the smaller steel companies and the hundreds of steel fabricators with whom the union had contracts. In 1956, 12 steel companies, representing 90 percent of U.S. steel production, agreed to form a joint industry committee.

McDonald presented his proposal for a guaranteed annual wage, known as Supplemental Unemployment Benefits (SUB), to the committee. It would provide that any employee who was laid off would receive his regular state-paid unemployment compensation, supplemented by the company, up to two-thirds of his regular earnings for up to one year. This was the primary goal of the 1956 negotiations, which also included a proposal for premium pay for weekend work. The talks were successful, and for the first time, steelworkers had a guaranteed annual wage. The union's Wage Policy Committee called the contract *"the greatest victory ever achieved by the United Steelworkers in its 20-year history."*

The 1959 2-B or Not 2-B Strike

In 1959, the steel companies decided to end, or at least modify, the union's workplace power through manpower rules. Most of the time, the rules that dictated how many men were needed for a particular job were not written down. They were known as *"past practice"* rules, developed over time and, under Section 2-B of the contract, could not be changed. Section 2-B stated that past practices concerning manning and work rules shall remain in effect for the duration of the contract. Management thought these practices were wasteful and expensive and an infringement on management's right to manage.[**see Appendix B-4 for the whole language of Section 2-B**] The confrontation between union and management over this issue led to the most significant labor strike in

American history. The strike ended as both a victory and a disaster.

Before the 1959 strike, the major American steel companies were reporting high profits, which led McDonald and Steelworkers general counsel Arthur J. Goldberg to request a significant wage increase. Industry negotiators refused to grant a wage increase unless McDonald agreed to a substantial alteration or an elimination of Section 2-B of the union's national master contract.

McDonald characterized management's proposals as an attempt to break the union. Negotiations broke off, and the contract expired on July 1, 1959.

President Eisenhower asked both sides to extend the agreement and resume bargaining. McDonald and Goldberg offered to extend the contract by one year. They also proposed creating a joint committee to study changes to Section 2-B and to the contract's benefit structure. Steelmakers rejected the offer.

On July 15th, 500,000 steelworkers went on strike. The strike shuttered nearly every steel mill in the country. By the end of August, the Department of Defense voiced concern that there would not be enough steel to meet national defense needs in a crisis.

Guards closing the gates to U.S. Steel at Gary.

York Times.

L.TE CITY EDITION

EDNESDAY, JULY 15, 1959. FIVE CENTS

STEEL STRIKE BEGINS, MILLS SHUT; LENGTHY WALKOUT IS PREDICTED; TALKS SET ON PRESIDENT'S PLEA

BID BY EISENHOWER

He Says Goodwill on Both Sides Could Speed Accord

By RICHARD E. MOONEY

Special to The New York Times.

WASHINGTON, July 14—President Eisenhower recommended late this afternoon that steel industry management and labor representatives immediately call on Federal mediators for assistance in reaching a contract agreement.

Both sides agreed within the hour to meet tomorrow with Joseph F. Finnegan, director of the Federal Mediation and Conciliation service.

With the strike deadline only hours away, President Eisenhower expressed "keen disappointment" over the negotiators' failure to reach agreement. He said that expiration of their contract "does not in any way relieve the parties of responsibility to continue to bargain without interruption."

Speedy Accord Urged

The Mediation Service provides a medium for continued talk. The service can only seek

SPURS PICKETING: David J. McDonald, president of United Steelworkers, raising placard bearing local's number last night at United States Steel Corporation's Fairless Works in Morrisville, Pa., just before strike began.

SESSION ON TODAY

Negotiators to Meet Here With Finnegan —500,000 Affected

Texts of union and industry statements are on Page 36.

By A. H. RASKIN

A half-million steel workers struck at 12:01 A. M. today. The walkout cut off production of 85 per cent of the country's basic industrial metal and threatened to slow the upsurge of the economy from last year's crippling recession.

Peace talks initiated by President Eisenhower collapsed at 2:15 P. M. yesterday, with each side blaming the other for the shutdown. The President immediately ordered the Federal Mediation and Conciliation Service to seek a speedy termination of the walkout.

Leaders of the United Steelworkers of America and the twelve biggest steel producers arranged to hold separate meetings this afternoon with Joseph F. Finnegan, the director of the service. But the total inability of the parties to make any

The New York Times announced the beginning of the strike.

The AFL-CIO quickly began to pressure McDonald to end the strike. Its president, George Meany, was willing to support the strike only if it did not affect national security negatively. The strike was also affecting the auto industry, which was threatening to lay off tens of thousands of UAW members due to a steel shortage.

On September 28, 1959, Eisenhower met privately with McDonald and Goldberg and threatened to invoke the Taft-Hartley Act's back-to-work provisions. McDonald was unwilling to budge on Section 2-B without other concessions from the steelmakers. The steel companies, realizing that they could wait until Eisenhower forced union members back to work, refused to make any such concessions.

Eisenhower set in motion the Taft-Hartley machinery on October 7th and appointed a Board of Inquiry. However, Eisenhower limited the Board's mandate to clarifying the issues rather than recommending a settlement. Realizing that the strike could linger despite the use of the Taft-Hartley provisions, management offered a three-year contract with small pay and fringe benefit increases and binding arbitration over Section 2-B. McDonald rejected the offer. He proposed a contract similar to his early July proposal, but reduced the union's wage and benefit demands and limited the contract to two rather than three years. Working from a plan devised by Goldberg, McDonald also proposed a nine-member committee consisting of three members from labor, management, and the public to study and resolve work-rule issues. Management rejected the new proposal.

On October 20th, the Department of Justice petitioned the federal district court for western Pennsylvania for a Taft-Hartley injunction ordering the steelworkers back to work. Goldberg argued that the Taft-Hartley Act was unconstitutional, but the district court ruled in favor of the government on October 21st.The United States Supreme Court set the argument for November 3, 1959.

On November 7, 1959, on the 116th day of the strike, the Supreme Court upheld the appellate court's findings. In *Steelworkers v. United States*, 361 U.S. 39 (1959), in an 8–1 decision, the court upheld the constitutionality of the Taft-Hartley Act. The justices affirmed the district court's injunction, ordering the workers back to work for an 80-day cooling-off period.

Union papers promoting the strike

McDonald reluctantly ordered his members back to work, but productivity slowed due to poor relationships between workers and managers. The Taft-Hartley Act required management to make a final offer and for union members to vote on it. Management proposed minimal wage and benefit improvements, as well as the elimination of Section 2-B. McDonald turned management of the union over to Goldberg to concentrate the legal and bargaining work in one set of hands. Goldberg convinced the union's leadership to reject the proposal.

Rejecting the contract was a dangerous tactic and could have broken the union if not for the support of Vice President Richard Nixon. Nixon planned to run for president in 1960 and offered his services in hopes of negotiating a settlement that might win him labor's backing.

In December, Nixon met privately with the steelmakers and cautioned them that the Democratic Congress would soon begin hearings on the steel strike. Neither Republicans nor Democrats would support the steel companies if the strike triggered an election-year recession, and Nixon urged management to accept the terms of the Kaiser Steel contract, which had settled separately. Industry executives agreed to a new contract in the last week of December.

On January 15, a new 20-month contract was signed. Section 2-B was preserved. Workers received a 7-cent-per-hour pay increase (61 cents in 2025 dollars), which was far lower than anything McDonald had demanded. For the first time, however, the union won an automatic cost-of-living wage adjustment and greatly improved pension and health benefits. McDonald trumpeted the settlement as a great victory, compared to what might have happened.

In the long run, the strike sparked a prolonged decline in the American steel industry. More than 85 percent of

U.S. steel production had been shut down for almost four months. Hungry for steel, American industries began importing it. Steel imports had been negligible before 1959. But during the strike, basic U.S. industries found Japanese and Korean steel to be less costly than American steel even after accounting for importation costs. Steel imports, which were less than two percent before the strike, jumped to five percent in the year following and were over 19 percent by 1981.

After the strike, steel consumers also began looking for substitutes for steel, such as plastics and aluminum. These shifts set in motion the gradual decline of the American basic steel industry.

The strike also eventually ended McDonald's tenure as president of the Steelworkers. Eager to avoid a repetition of the 1959 strike, McDonald worked with steel industry executives to widen the mandate of the new nine-member commissions (now known as "Human Relations Committees"). A three-year national steel contract was signed on March 31, 1962. The union agreed not to enforce Section 2-B and permitted increased automation, with a percentage of the profits from automation going to wage increases. However, union members began to feel McDonald was not protecting their interests.

4 Union Democracy Fires Break Out

The Dues Protest Committee

Fresh off of what the union's Wage Policy Committee called "the greatest contract in history," the Steelworkers met for their biannual national convention in 1956.The union now represented 1,200,000 workers and had a staff of 1,200. The International Executive Board recommended increasing dues from $3 a month to $5 a month ($47 in 2025 dollars). They also recommended a salary increase for staff, including raising the presidential salary from $40,000 to $50,000 a year ($470,000).When this proposal was put to a vote on the convention floor, a voice vote was not definitive, but on a standing vote, it was declared passed, but the vote was close. There were demands for a roll call vote, but McDonald refused. The mood of revolt was in the air. Never had there been such dissent at a Steelworkers convention. Although the protest lost, it would form a core of opposition that would lead to the first contested presidential election in the union's history.

The face of what became known as the Dues Protest Committee (DPC) was Donald Rarick, a mill worker and union grievance committee member at U.S. Steel Irvin Works in McKeesport, Pennsylvania. Behind the scenes, District Director William Hart from Pittsburgh was providing expert help. Initially, the DPC wanted to persuade enough local unions to petition for a special convention to reconsider the dues increase. The DPC was centered in the Pittsburgh area, so it was challenging to communicate with other locals nationally. The International Union controlled all local union contact information. Helping in the effort was the local press in mill towns, which ran many stories on the issue. A special convention call needed support from 700 locals, but only 100 officially petitioned, including the two most prominent locals, Local 1014 in Gary, Indiana, and Local 1211 in Aliquippa, Pennsylvania.

Having failed with the special convention petition request, the DPC decided to run candidates for president and other top positions. A couple of District Directors turned down the opportunity to run, so the DPC decided to run Rarick. In 1956, the union constitution required a candidate for international office to get nominations from at least 40 locals out of 2,800 local unions to be placed on the ballot. The DPC drive received enough support to give Rarick 91 nominations against McDonald's 1,905. Mill town newspapers gave this news front-page coverage.

The First Contested Election

The contest was one-sided. McDonald had the command of the union establishment and staff. He called six regional conferences composed of local union officers and staff members from different parts of the country. McDonald used these conferences to counter the rapidly growing Rarick movement. They cost the union $1 million. *Steel Labor,* which was mailed to every member, praised McDonald but did not mention Rarick or that the first contested presidential election was about to occur.

As the votes were counted, credible charges of vote fraud emerged. One staff representative said later, *"We worked overtime, got tired of marking ballots late into the night to make sure McDonald came out of our district with a respectable majority."* At Local 1014 in Gary, which had backed the dues protest petition, Rarick claimed to have won 9,000 to 3,000. The vote count reported to the International was reversed, giving McDonald the victory. At one polling place in Clarendon, Pennsylvania, the local threw the ballots out. The McDonald supporters got some new unnumbered ballots and marked them. A member found the old ones and dumped them on the lawn of a local attorney who took up Rarick's later appeal. When the official results were announced, McDonald had 404,000 votes and Rarick had 223,500.McDonald had failed to beat a previously unknown local union leader by even a two-to-one margin.

The McClellan Committee

Robert F. Kennedy, McClellan Committee General Counsel.

Apparent vote fraud may have contributed to McDonald's victory, but it set in motion legislation that would affect the operations of every union. Rarick and other leaders of the DPC protested to the McClellan Committee. The McClellan Committee (officially known as the United States Senate Select Committee on Improper Activities in Labor and Management) had been set up to investigate the extent of criminal or other improper practices in the field of labor-management relations or in unions or employers, and to suggest changes in the laws of the United States that would protect such practices or activities. Robert F. Kennedy was General Counsel of the Committee, and he sent letters to all the Steelworker locals to retain their ballots.

Allegations about the use of union funds flew back and forth, and the investigation lasted several months. Although the investigation did not reach any specific conclusion, the committee felt legislation was needed to curb union power abuses in elections and ensure some membership rights. Rarick was elected to be president of his local union, and other DPC leaders were elected to leadership in their locals over the opposition of McDonald.

In 1972, steelworker members from Local 1462 in Youngstown, Ohio, summed up the Due Protest Committee:

JOHN BARBERO: Every other major steelworker local had experiences like ours – dishonest elections and absolutely no rights on the job. The thing that impressed me was that the dues increase was insignificant. It was the straw that tied everything together. Dishonest elections, no on-the-job representation, no voice – everything that everybody felt.

ED MANN:I don't think it was a greedy thing. People resented the international union asking for more money. We don't have the right to strike; so why build up a big strike and defense fund for the international union, when local problems are not being taken care of?

JOHN BARBERO: Even so, we won some victories with the dues protest. McDonald was taking us down quite a road. The dues protest is a reason the Steelworkers is a little freer organization today. We were part of the same pressure that was building up within the Teamsters, with the Mineworkers, everywhere else. For democracy.

Through it came the Landrum-Griffin bill. I don't know, maybe the labor bureaucrats are right in saying it's anti-union like the Taft-Hartley, but as far as on-the-job democracy is concerned, this is the first breath of fresh air that came into the trade union movement.

Jimmy Hoffa, Teamsters President, confronting Robert Kennedy at the McClellan Committee hearings.

The Landrum-Griffin Act

As a result of the investigation into the Steelworkers' election and other union investigations, Congress enacted the Landrum-Griffin Act. This law affected the internal life of the American trade-union movement to an unprecedented degree. Two of its sections mainly affected the United Steelworkers:

1) Its *"Bill of Rights for Union Members"* [**see Appendix B-3**] and 2) its section on *"Elections"*. It provided rules and standards governing increases in dues and assessments, and forbade any labor organization from *"limiting the right of any member to institute an action in any court or appear as a witness"* in any proceeding. Except that he may be required to exhaust reasonable hearing procedures (but not to exceed four months) within such organization, before instituting legal or administrative proceedings against such organization or any other officer thereof. Also, *"no interested employer or employer association shall directly or indirectly finance, encourage, or participate in, except as a party, any such action, proceeding, appearance or petition."*

In the conduct of a union election, the law (officially the *Labor-Management Reporting and Disclosure Act of 1959*) spelled out in considerable detail the rights of candidates for union office and the obligation of the organizations to see that such rights are fulfilled. 29 U.S. Code § 481 has several sections that address the complaints made by the DPC.

Section (c) **Distribution of Campaign Literature** states: *a labor organization has to comply with all reasonable requests of any candidate to distribute by mail or otherwise at the candidate's expense campaign* *literature in aid of such person's candidacy to all members in good standing of such labor organization and to refrain from discrimination in favor of or against any candidate with respect to the use of lists of members, and whenever such labor organizations or its officers authorize the distribution by mail or otherwise to members of campaign literature on behalf of any candidate or of the labor organization itself with reference to such election, similar distribution at the request of any other bona fide candidate shall be made by such labor organization and its officers, with equal treatment as to the expense of such distribution.*

Section (e) **Conduct of Elections** states: *In any election required by this section which is to be held by secret ballot a reasonable opportunity shall be given for the nomination of candidates and every member in good standing shall be eligible to be a candidate and to hold office (subject to section 504 of this title and to reasonable qualifications uniformly imposed) and shall have the right to vote for or otherwise support the candidate or candidates of his choice, without being subject to penalty, discipline, or improper interference or reprisal of any kind by such organization or any member thereof. Not less than fifteen days prior to the election, notice thereof shall be mailed to each member at his last known home address. Each member in good standing shall be entitled to one vote. No member whose dues have been withheld by his employer for payment to such organization* *pursuant to his voluntary authorization provided for in a collective bargaining agreement shall be declared ineligible to vote or be a candidate for office in such organization by reason of alleged delay or default in the payment of dues. The votes cast by members of each local labor organization shall be counted, and the results published, separately. The election officials designated in the constitution and bylaws, or the secretary, if no other official is designated, shall preserve for one year the ballots and all other records pertaining to the election.*

Finally, Section (g) **Use of Dues or Employer Funds to Promote a Candidate** states: *No money received by any labor organization by way of dues, assessment, or similar levy, and no money of an employer shall be contributed or applied to promote the candidacy of any person in any election, subject to the provisions of this subchapter. Such monies of a labor organization may be utilized for notices, factual statements of issues not involving candidates, and other expenses necessary for the holding of an election.*

This law would be used by opposition activists not only in Steelworker elections but in other unions to this day.

1965: The Closest Election

In 1965, the Steelworkers Union would see an inter-headquarters battle and its closest Presidential election. Iorwith Wilbur Abel (commonly known as I.W. Abel) began working at 17 in 1925 as a molder for the American

Sheet and Tin Plate Company (now U.S. Steel) in Canton. He often switched jobs and worked at the Canton Malleable Iron Company, the Timken Roller Bearing Company, and the Colonial Foundry.

Laid off during the Great Depression, Abel worked at a brickmaking company, loading a kiln, for less than a quarter of his former pay. Convinced that a union would have protected him from losing his job, he became active in the American labor movement.

In 1936, Abel found work again at Timken Roller Bearing and, with the assistance of the Steel Workers Organizing Committee (SWOC), he organized Steel Workers Local 1123. He remained a member of the local until his death. He proved to be an effective and strong negotiator and union president, and in one year alone, he led 42 wildcat strikes.

I.W. Abel 1908 – 1987.

Abel was an active participant in the Little Steel Strike in 1937. His skilled leadership during the strike brought him to the attention of national SWOC officers and staff.

In 1937, Abel was hired by SWOC to head the national union's organizing staff. Abel became a protégé of Philip Murray, president of SWOC. When the United Steel Workers was formed in 1942, Abel was appointed director of the Canton District of the USW. For the next ten years, Abel led Steelworker Union organizing drives. During World War II, Abel served on the National War Labor Board, representing the Congress of Industrial Organizations (CIO).

When Murray died in 1952 and Secretary-Treasurer David J. McDonald was elected president as his successor, Abel was elected Secretary-Treasurer. Unlike the flamboyant and vocal McDonald, Abel remained in the background as the union's Secretary-Treasurer. He was appointed to the CIO-PAC, the CIO's political action committee. He spent most of his time visiting local unions and listening to members.

In the early 1960s, Abel was angered by what he perceived as McDonald's weakness in securing new national steelworker contracts. As a result of the 1959 strike settlement, McDonald and steel management formed the Human Relations Committee (HRC). Increasingly, this committee had taken over the union's

Wage Policy Committee's role in contract negotiations. Otis Brubaker, the former head of research for the union, put it this way:

In 1962, there was at least the pretense of going through the procedures of the union's Wage Policy Committee before the early settlement, even though its recommendations were almost totally ignored in the settlement. In 1963, the pretense was dropped. No Wage Policy Committee was even called. The HRC became an open substitute for the union's regular procedures. There were no open demands. No use was made of the union's bargaining power. A deal was made in secret HRC sessions... What happened in 1963 was not collective bargaining. It was collective begging.

The 1963 settlement won praise from the *Wall Street Journal* as *"the lowest cost settlement since 1944."Iron Age* said, *"This contract made a success of the Human Relations Committee...a triumph of Human Relations bargaining."*

Brubaker commented, *"This is quite an endorsement – and all from industry sources. With a few more such triumphs, we could lose the entire war—and our union as well."* Brubaker stated, *"Under the HRC, the union has achieved the following:*

1. *Two of the cheapest settlements in our union's postwar history.*
2. *'Real' wage cuts for our members.*
3. *Secret dealing by a palace clique instead of collective bargaining.*
4. *Bypassing of our union's Wage Policy Committee.*
5. *Deliberate and determined non-usage of the union's only bargaining power—the threat to strike, if all other recourse fails, in support of its demands.*

"This is no good," Brubaker declared, *"This whole HRC mutual trusteeship is alien to all that is good within the trade union movement. It must be destroyed."*

Increasingly, many of the union's District directors, especially those with large numbers of basic steel members, came to agree with Brubaker's position. Some of them, led by the leader of the union's largest district, Joe Germano in Chicago, urged Abel to run against McDonald in 1965.

After McDonald pushed through a change to the union's constitution in 1964 that permitted him to serve two more four-year terms, Abel decided to challenge McDonald in the 1965 presidential election. Abel accused McDonald of being too cozy with employers by substituting fringe benefit gains for wage increases and ignoring members' concerns. Abel received 1,533 nominations from locals, and McDonald received 1,048.The election took place on February 9, 1965. Voting irregularities and challenged ballots delayed a final result until April 30. Abel relied heavily on voting and ballot-challenging procedures established under the relatively new Landrum-Griffin Act. Without the new law's assistance, it is unclear whether he would have won.

However, union officials and federal monitors eventually declared that Abel had received 308,910 votes and McDonald 298,768, giving Abel a razor-thin margin of 10,142 votes. McDonald declined to challenge the result. Over 7,000 of the votes came from Canadian locals, and Abel spent more time than any of his predecessors protecting the interests of Canadian steelworker locals. Abel was sworn in as USWA president on June 2, 1965.

Abel's Reign: Reform and Reaction

During Abel's presidency, membership in the USWA rose by more than 500,000, as he engineered mergers with the International Union of Mine, Mill, and Smelter Workers in 1967; the United Stone and Allied Product Workers of America in 1971; and District 50 of the Allied and Technical Workers of America in 1972.

Abel actively sought new federal laws to protect union workers as well. He was a vigorous proponent of workplace health and safety and worked to help pass the Occupational Safety and Health Act in 1970. He was also a strong advocate of the Employee Retirement

Income Security Act of 1974, which protected the interests of participants in private pension plans and established the Pension Benefit Guaranty Corporation.

Abel also won several strong national steel and other metals contracts. He established the union's first strike fund and quickly amassed an $85 million balance. He resumed coordinated bargaining with the major steelmakers and established separate bargaining councils for aluminum and other metals industries.

Abel also broadened the union's inclusiveness. He encouraged open discussion of controversial issues among the staff and membership and decentralized several union functions. He also worked to increase minority participation in local, regional, and national union affairs and to end job discrimination by local steelworker unions.

Abel faced a challenger of his own in 1969. Emil Narick, an unknown staff attorney, received 41 percent of the total vote. More importantly, he got 63 percent of the votes from the large steel mills. This contest opened many eyes in the opposition. It looked like the 'right guy' could actually win the presidency.

The Steel Industry Changes in the 1970s

Changes that had begun in the 1960s took firm hold in the 1970s. New technology was reducing the number of workers needed to produce a ton of steel. There was an aggressive attempt by foreign steel producers to destroy domestic steel production. Out-of-country steel companies are subsidized by their home governments and can 'dump' their steel into the U.S. market below the cost of production. This caused the domestic producers to lose customers, often permanently. Mini-mills, which produce steel by melting down recycled steel, came on the scene and took market share from the large legacy steel mills. The mini-mills have much lower costs since they do not have the costly 'front' of an integrated mill, which consists of coke ovens, blast furnaces, and a melt shop that produces virgin steel. They have lower labor costs because they tend to be non-union and do not have the enormous legacy pension costs that the older companies had. Finally, many of the large steel mills started investing in other industries. U.S. Steel, for example, bought Marathon Oil and became known as USX for a time. All of these changes had a significant effect on the union. It became more diversified as it gained members in other industries but lost them in basic steel.

The National Ad Hoc Committee

The National Ad Hoc Committee was a Chicago-area group established in 1964 in Detroit by Black steelworker activists from local unions in East Chicago, Gary, and Chicago. The International Executive Board, consisting of the president, vice president, and secretary-treasurer, plus the 30 district directors, had always been all white since the union's inception. No one running for national office had ever slated an African American for office. Although the union was about 20% black, there were fewer than 100 black staff members out of more than 1,500 nationwide. In the districts, there was only one sub-district director.

The Ad Hoc Committee felt they had encountered Jim Crow unionism for too long. They charged that local unions had worked with the companies to draw up lines of progression that excluded blacks from getting top positions or jobs where blacks could go into the crafts.

In the 1965 election between McDonald and Abel, the Committee gave three demands to the candidates: 1) the reorganization of the Civil Rights Committee into a full-scale department headed by an African American; 2) more black representation on staff in the districts and nationally; and 3) the inclusion of an African American on the International Executive Board. Abel committed to some of the demands, and the northern black vote put Abel over the top in a very close election.

The alliance between the new President Abel and the Ad Hoc Committee did not last long. Abel did not press the district directors on adding black staff. The Committee decided to picket the International Convention in Chicago in August 1968. This demonstration attracted media attention and caused the union leadership much embarrassment.

Muggy

Sidelined

THE TIMES

Home Newspaper of the Calumet Region

Vol. LXIII No. 54 — Hammond-East Chicago, Indiana; Calumet City-Lansing, Illinois, Tuesday, August 20, 1968 — 3 Sections—10c

USW Blacks Ask Voice

Ad Hoc Committee demonstrates at the 1968 Convention

Abel Promises: No Concession to Blacks

I. W. Abel, president of the United Steelworkers of America, said yesterday that no special consideration will be given to Negroes in filling vacancies on the executive board or in high union offices. The steelworkers national convention will open today in Donovan hall in the International Amphitheater.

I. W. Abel

Dissident Negro union members have asked the union's 32-member executive board to create positions for them and have threatened to picket the convention if their demands are not met.

Free to Seek Offices

Abel, in a press conference in the Pick-Congress hotel, said the protesting Negro union members have been told that they are free to seek high union offices in democratic elections, but no special considerations will be given to them.

him on whether he is going to come to Chicago."

George Meany, AFL-CIO president, and Bayard Rustin, executive director of the A. Phillip Randolph institute, will speak at the convention tomorrow, and W. Willard Wirtz,

Abel's response to the Ad Hoc demonstration

The Ad Hoc Committee continued to agitate to desegregate the International Union at the national and district levels. The committee allied with other groups as issues of union democracy, the right to strike, and the right to ratify contracts took hold in the early 1970s. These groups allied to form Steelworkers Fightback, as discussed below. The Ad Hoc Committee disbanded in the face of the larger multiracial group. Its leaders credited the committee with taking on the International and integrating it to at least some degree. They also credited the committee with the Consent Decree in 1974.

The Consent Decree

Social protests of the 1960s spilled into the workplaces. Workers sued the union for race and sex discrimination numerous times in the late 1960s and early 1970s. Using huge defense contracts, the federal government was able to use that tool to pressure steel mills to hire more women and African Americans. The steel companies had long discriminated against blacks and other minority workers. It started with hiring, where blacks were often sent to the dirty and physically most demanding parts of the mill. These were the 'front-end' of the mills; departments like the Coke Ovens, Blast Furnace, Melt Shops, and Primary Rolling Mills. Whites often started at the cleaner Finishing Mills or in the higher-paying skilled crafts. Through the years, the union had done little to change these practices, and the contract had institutionalized this discrimination with what was known as department seniority. Job promotions were based on a worker's departmental seniority, not overall plant seniority. This made it difficult to transfer to open jobs in cleaner departments. Also, if someone was making a high rate of pay in an undesirable area, he would have to give that up to go to the bottom pay of a better area.

As a result, many complaints and lawsuits against both the companies and the union were filed with the U.S. Department of Labor and the Equal Employment Opportunity Commission. In 1974, the USW and the steel companies signed a consent decree to alter seniority rules that discriminated against women and minority workers. It also ordered $31 million ($162 million in 2025 dollars) in back pay for victims of discriminatory hiring and promotions. The back pay went to more than 40,000 black, Spanish-surnamed, and women workers hired before 1968. They received awards from $250 ($1300) to upwards of $3000 ($15,650).

The Decree ordered that full plant seniority be used for promotions in a department. Job openings in departments had to be posted throughout the mill so people could bid on them. If a worker successfully bid into another department, he would not lose his current rate of pay for two years. Openings in craft apprenticeships were to be posted in the plant so all could bid on them.

This Decree was intended to address past discrimination, but it sparked significant dissension within the union. Many were angered that they had lost their department seniority and that 'outsiders' had moved past them. Racism affected many in the crafts who did not want minorities to be part of their jobs. The bonus given to minorities angered those who did not get it. The union did not handle any of this well since its own practices had furthered the discrimination. This dissension only increased when the layoffs of the late 1970s and 1980s were made by plant seniority, and departments had to be reduced.

Jack Parton, who became District 31 Director in 1981, said:

There was a lot of discrimination at Gary Works, not just racial but also in terms of nationalities. This Greek superintendent, for instance, would try to get mainly Greeks and Serbians. When I hired in, 13 of us from Virginia all went to Number 4 open hearth. A month and a half later, I was probably the only one left. The others all packed up and went back. Blacks went to the Coke plant. Some of those jobs, when you start at the bottom, are dirty and nasty.

While I was a grievance committeeman, we changed the way people were promoted. Suddenly, everyone had the opportunity. Previously, people could be in dead-end jobs forever because if you transferred to a different unit, you kept your pension and vacation rights but lost seniority. Hell, they gave people off the streets better jobs than people who'd been there 20 years.It was a much-needed reform.

Flyer for the Jack Parton and the Unity Slate at Local 1014 Gary Works

The Consent Decree was effectively challenged in court in 1974. A worker at Kaiser Aluminum was denied a promotion due to a company and union agreement to allow blacks and whites into a training program on a one-to-one basis, even though there were many more whites than blacks at the plant. The U.S. Supreme Court ruled in *United Steelworkers v. Weber* in 1979 that the affirmative action plan was lawful. The court said Title VII of the Civil Rights Act did not bar employers from favoring women and minorities in order to remedy past discrimination.

Experimental Negotiating Agreement

In 1971, record imports of foreign steel led to 108,000 steelworkers being laid off. Although a new national steel contract was reached without a strike the same year, Abel and the USWA executive council realized that the steel industry's tendency to stockpile steel in anticipation of a strike led to a boom-and-bust cycle, which hurt workers.

To counteract the cycle, in 1973, Abel negotiated the Experimental Negotiating Agreement (ENA) with the major steelmakers. The union agreed not to strike during the 1974 contract talks and agreed to arbitration for any bargaining issues that led to an impasse.

The ENA proved a success during the 1974 national steel contract talks. The union won a $2.00 an hour raise ($10.40 in 2025 dollars) over three years. Included was a $150 ($800) bonus for every steelworker covered by the contract. The union also won the right to engage in local strikes over non-economic working conditions, which the union had agreed to ban in previous agreements. The pay increase caught the steelworkers up with the autoworkers, which had long been a goal of the USW.

The ENA became controversial as mills began to shut down in the mid-1970s due to imported steel. Rank and file groups around the country began to organize against its renewal. Union opposition was angry that the ENA was sprung on the membership without warning. Members were not allowed a vote. The average member felt disenfranchised by the union hierarchy. Although wages increased because of a cost-of-living provision in the inflation-riddled 1970s, many thought it was a 'sellout' at the time. Future District 31 Director Jack Parton said:

I came down on the side of ENA. We made significant wage gains. If we could go back in time, I wouldn't support ENA. If people don't have to fight, they become complacent and don't understand why they need a labor movement. The company pounded away that, "We're giving you this." Shit, they gave it in return for the no-strike assurance.

Various rank-and-file groups sued the USW in federal court in Pittsburgh. The lawsuit asked that the parties be enjoined from implementing the ENA. The complaint argued the Steelworkers' constitution guaranteed the right to strike and could not be given up without a complete democratic process. The complaint said the ENA was negotiated in private and then presented to the union's ratifying committee with no advance notice. The judge ruled against the rank-and-file committee, but in return for not appealing, the companies gave up some concessions.

1960s Protests Spill into the Workplace

As the 1960s ended, the student and social protest movements started to find traction in the nation's workplaces, especially with younger workers. Many workers wanted a say in how their job was done or how their union was run. Movements for union democracy sprang up in many industries, including auto, mines, and the Teamsters. In the Mine Workers, Jock Yablonski, a reform opponent to the corrupt head of the UMW, Tony Boyle, was murdered in 1969. The Miners for Democracy was formed and successfully ran Arnold Miller for President in 1972. They were able to use the legal muscle of the Labor Department to have a fair election. In steel, some activists thought the government could be of help to ensure a fair election since there had been fraud in the past.

The mills were hiring many young people in the late 1960s and early 1970s because the immediate post-World War II hires were retiring. These new workers had seen anti-war protests and carried anti-authoritarian trends into the mill. Also, many leftist organizers went into the mills in this period following the break-up of Students for a Democratic Society. They were trying to organize industrial workers and formed various rank-and-file caucuses in their local unions.

In the midst of this growing opposition to the International Union, a vocal dissenter from Chicago stepped up to challenge the union's establishment in 1973 when District 31 director Joe Germano announced his retirement.

The Chicago-Gary area was the center of steelworker insurgency in the 1970s. Previous centers in Pittsburgh and Youngstown had faded as mills closed. New mills were opening in District 31 as Inland Steel continued to expand, and Bethlehem Steel opened the newest steel mill in the U.S. at Burns Harbor, Indiana, just east of Gary.

The Rebel on the Staff

Ed Sadlowski 1938 – 2018.

In 1956, Edward Sadlowski started work as a machinist's apprentice at the U.S. Steel Southworks mill in Chicago, represented by Local 65 of the United Steelworkers. He got his nickname "Oil can Eddie" because he often carried an oil can while walking around buildings at the mill, putting oil on machines where needed, and talking with members. Ed has grown up in a steelworker family. His father helped organize Inland Steel in East Chicago, Indiana, with the SWOC. Fellow workers elected Sadlowski shop steward of his plant in 1960 and their grievance representative in 1962. The following year, Local 65 members elected him their president over a four-term incumbent. In 1964, at age 25, Sadlowski became the youngest person to hold that union office, representing about 10,000 workers. He won re-election in 1967. Chicago District 31 Director Joe Germano appointed Sadlowski to the International Union staff in 1970.

When Germano announced he was going to retire, he said he was supporting Sam Evett, his office assistant, to replace him. Evett had never worked in a steel mill. Activists saw this as a chance to put a reformer into leadership. Sadlowski released a statement:

I consider union democracy to be the most important single issue. If the steelworkers had been consulted, they would have never agreed to an International Executive Board that excluded blacks, Latinos, and women. If the steelworkers were consulted, they would insist on their right to vote on union contracts in the same manner as other unions do. They rightfully feel they are not running their own affairs and are not being appropriately represented on the district level.

The Sadlowski campaign was conducted at plant gates, bars, and restaurants. He surrounded himself with a network of old union activists and some younger people who had the energy to leaflet the gates at shift changes. District 31 was wrapped around Lake Michigan, and steelworkers were not only at steel mills but also at foundries, can makers, machine shops, and other manufacturing facilities in the area. On the West side of Chicago alone, there were 500 small parts plants represented by the union. There were 130,000 steelworker members—the most in the union—in a relatively small area. Many leftwing groups sent people to help in the campaign. The help was accepted as long as it was limited to handing out leaflets. Sadlowski and those around him were afraid of red-baiting. Some of those closest to him, such as Jim and Clem Balanoff, had been members of the Communist Party. Most left groups, which are known for ideological purity tests, seemed to put those differences aside while they were involved in the campaign.

Sadlowski's first job was to get on the ballot. This required the nominations from at least 29 local unions out of 297 in the district. The International Union would not give Sadlowski any contact information for the local unions. Fortunately, a retired staffman, Stanley Righten, who did not like Germano, supplied Sadlowski with a list of every plant and its location, plus who was there at what time. The list was invaluable.

The steel companies allowed Evett to come inside plants and mills to campaign. Germano caused voting places for some locals to be moved up to two miles away. Despite the roadblocks, the Sadlowski campaign distributed over a million and a half pieces of literature and held rallies all over a district that ran from Skokie, Illinois, to South Bend, Indiana.

The election occurred on February 13, 1973. As the votes were reported from locals around the district, Sadlowski was several thousand votes ahead by nightfall.

But the two prominent U.S. Steel Gary locals had not reported. These locals had a history of vote fraud allegations. Sadlowski's observer at Local 1066 had not shown up, claiming death threats. At Local 1014, the numbered ballots were not issued in sequence to voters, making it difficult to account for ballots. Local 1066 reported their vote as 935 to 239 in favor of Evett. Local 1014 reported 1,720 to 365 in Evett's favor. These vote totals were opposite the pattern of the other big mills in the district. At Republic Steel's Chicago plant, Sadlowski got 454 to 329; the Bethlehem Steel local voted 639 to 335 for Sadlowski; U.S. Steel Southworks voted for Sadlowski 1,346 to 447; and Inland Steel's local gave Sadlowski the win 3,535 to 1,910. When the Gary locals reported it was enough to put Evett over the top. He claimed a victory of a 2,350 vote margin out of 47,856 cast.

New Election Ordered

Sadlowski used the procedures established by the Landrum-Griffin Act to appeal to the U.S. Department of Labor. The FBI was brought in and found hundreds of identical ballots marked with the same pencil. Other instances of fraud were found. At Local 1066, President Danny Cefalia had locked a room and, with two others, signed hundreds of ballots and stuffed the ballot box.

Future District 31 director Jack Parton said:

The vote fraud went beyond Local 1014.I went to the hearings in Chicago, not as a witness but just as an observer. Clearly, Eddie's allegations of hanky panky had some truth to them. Ultimately, the International agreed to a second election. I think if the original election had been honest, it would have been close. I don't know that Eddie would have won.

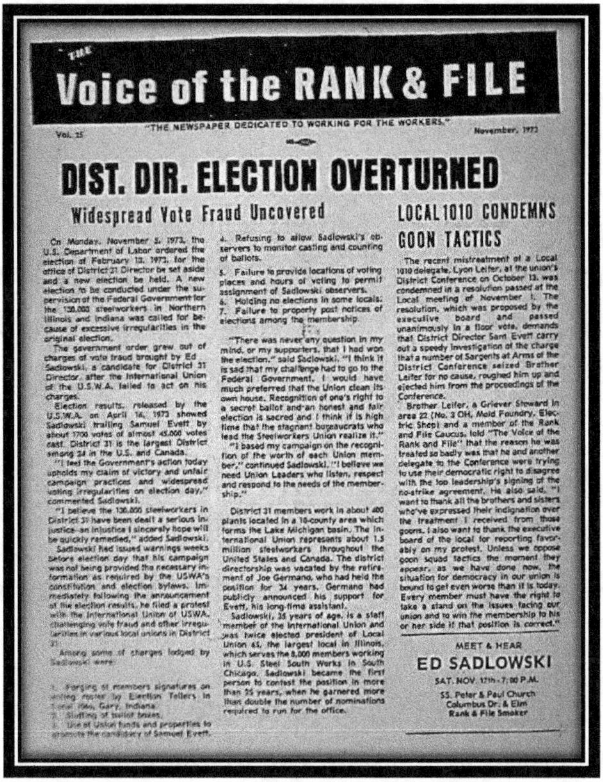

THE Voice of the RANK & FILE

"THE NEWSPAPER DEDICATED TO WORKING FOR THE WORKERS."

Vol. 25 — November, 1973

DIST. DIR. ELECTION OVERTURNED

Widespread Vote Fraud Uncovered

On Monday, November 5, 1973, the U.S. Department of Labor ordered the election of February 13, 1973, for the office of District 31 Director be set aside and a new election be held. A new election to be conducted under the supervision of the Federal Government for the 130,000 steelworkers in Northern Illinois and Indiana was called for because of excessive irregularities in the original election.

The government order grew out of charges of vote fraud brought by Ed Sadlowski, a candidate for District 31 Director, after the International Union of the U.S.W.A. failed to act on his charges.

Election results, released by the U.S.W.A. on April 16, 1973 showed Sadlowski trailing Samuel Evett by about 1700 votes of almost 45,000 votes cast. District 31 is the largest District among 24 in the U.S. and Canada.

"I feel the Government's action today upholds my claim of victory and unfair campaign practices and widespread voting irregularities on election day," commented Sadlowski.

"I believe the 130,000 steelworkers in District 31 have been dealt a serious injustice—an injustice I sincerely hope will be quickly remedied," added Sadlowski.

Sadlowski had issued warnings weeks before election day that his campaign was not being provided the necessary information as required by the USWA's constitution and election bylaws. Immediately following the announcement of the election results, he filed a protest with the International Union of USWA, challenging vote fraud and other irregularities in various local unions in District 31.

Among some of charges lodged by Sadlowski were:

1. Forging of members signatures on voting roster by Election Tellers in Local 1066, Gary, Indiana.
2. Stuffing of ballot boxes.
3. Use of Union funds and properties to promote the candidacy of Samuel Evett.
4. Refusing to allow Sadlowski's observers to monitor casting and counting of ballots.
5. Failure to provide locations of voting places and hours of voting to permit assignment of Sadlowski observers.
6. Holding no elections in some locals.
7. Failure to properly post notices of elections among the membership.

"There was never any question in my mind, or my supporters, that I had won the election," said Sadlowski. "I think it is sad that my challenge had to go to the Federal Government. I would have much preferred that the Union clean its own house. Recognition of one's right to a secret ballot and an honest and fair election is sacred and I think it is high time that the stagnant bureaucrats who lead the Steelworkers Union realize it."

"I based my campaign on the recognition of the worth of each Union member," continued Sadlowski. "I believe we need Union Leaders who listen, respect and respond to the needs of the membership."

District 31 members work in about 400 plants located in a 10-county area which forms the Lake Michigan basin. The International Union represents about 1.5 million steelworkers throughout the United States and Canada. The district directorship was vacated by the retirement of Joe Germano, who had held the position for 34 years. Germano had publicly announced his support for Evett, his long-time assistant.

Sadlowski, 35 years of age, is a staff member of the International Union and was twice elected president of Local Union 65, the largest local in Illinois, which serves the 8,000 members working in U.S. Steel South Works in South Chicago. Sadlowski became the first person to contest the position in more than 25 years, when he garnered more than double the number of nominations required to run for the office.

LOCAL 1010 CONDEMNS GOON TACTICS

The recent mistreatment of a Local 1010 delegate, Lyon Leifer, at the union's District Conference on October 13, was condemned in a resolution passed at the Local meeting of November 1. The resolution, which was proposed by the executive board and passed unanimously in a floor vote, demands that District Director Sam Evett carry out a speedy investigation of the charge that a number of Sargents at Arms of the District Conference seized Brother Leifer for no cause, roughed him up and ejected him from the proceedings of the Conference.

Brother Leifer, a Griever Steward in area 22 (No. 3 OH, Mold Foundry, Electric Shop) and a member of the Rank and File Caucus, told "The Voice of the Rank and File" that the reason he was treated so badly was that he and another delegate to the Conference were trying to use their democratic right to disagree with the top leadership's signing of the no-strike agreement. He also said, "I want to thank all the brothers and sisters who've expressed their indignation over the treatment I received from those goons. I also want to thank the executive board of the local for reporting favorably on my protest. Unless we oppose goon squad tactics the moment they appear, as we have done now, the situation for democracy in our union is bound to get even worse than it is today. Every member must have the right to take a stand on the issues facing our union and to win the membership to his or her side if that position is correct."

MEET & HEAR

ED SADLOWSKI

SAT. NOV. 17th - 7:00 P.M.

SS. Peter & Paul Church
Columbus Dr. & Elm
Rank & File Smoker

Newsletter distributed to the mills about the election.

The charges of fraud brought in labor lawyers like Joe Rauh, who had worked for Miners for Democracy. Chicago Alderman Leon Depres helped with the Labor Department appeal. Sadlowski submitted violations involving 147 of the district's 297 locals. After months of investigations, on November 5, 1973, the Justice

Department filed a suit for a new election. The suit alleged violations of the Landrum-Griffin Act specifically 1) Inadequate control of ballots and ballot boxes; 2) Failure to maintain proper eligibility and voter lists; 3) Allowing electioneering in polling places; 4) Denying candidates the right to have observers in polling places; 5) Failure to observe the rules of the union constitution and election manuals; and 6) Use of union funds to promote Evett's candidacy.

The International Union settled with the Justice Department and ordered a new election for November 12-15, 1974, under the supervision of the Department of Labor. Several hundred federal agents were brought in to conduct the election. Sadlowski's general theme was the corruption of the International. The campaign had helmet stickers which said *"Tell'em Again Ed"*.

The new vote was Sadlowski 39,637 to Evett's 20,058. The *Washington Post* said:

Inside observers saw this election as a possible stimulus for future challenges to incumbents. Moreover, neither Abel nor Secretary-Burke will be able to run for office again. The union constitution calls for compulsory retirement after 65. Should Sadlowski try for the presidency and win, it could mean a restructuring of the union as well as a more aggressive attitude in labor-management relations.

Sadlowski dismissed his own leadership role.

Our worst problem in organizing these campaigns is overcoming the mystique that the labor boss is some God. People would say to us, 'You can't go against Joe Germano or his man. He has been there since the union was started. They won't even let you get on the ballot.

So I get on the ballot. I won the first election, but they stole it on the count. The Labor Department comes in, and I win the rerun by two to one. Now I am ballyhooed as the 'new man of steel' in all the papers. This leads to the same mythical bullshit over again. If I start believing this, I'm in trouble.

When I went out for this thing, most steelworkers outside of South Chicago had never heard of me. The real game was in pounding the pavement in front of the plants, getting to know the members, finding tough campaigners who wouldn't fold under pressure, and understanding the issues in every part of this industry.

Preparing for the Next Fight

Sadlowski had little time to make plans for the next fight. He had become District Director of the union's largest district, but the next election was only two years away. He could either make peace with the 'Official Family' in Pittsburgh or start immediately to run for International president. Some wanted him to make a record as a director, which would take a term or two. The problem was that the International would have the power to appoint the staff so that they could freeze him out. On the other side, there was going to be an opening for president. Who knows when the next time that would happen? An International Union legislative lobbyist, Carl Alessi, said:

Sadlowski got elected as a rebel. The only way he can maintain that image is to keep the pot boiling. If he were to have called the staff together at the beginning and said, "Let's all pull together," he would have lost that image. They would have said he joined the administration.

Sadlowski with U.S. Steel Southworks in the background.

Sadlowski said:

I never want to be known as a labor statesman. The best feeling in the world is to break that chain they have around your neck, to step out without hesitancy or reservation when the issue is right.

When Sadlowski first came into the District 31 office in East Chicago, Indiana, he found all the files missing. His staff was cut from 60 to 43, and his opponent, Sam Evett, was appointed by Abel as "Midwest coordinator." It was clear there would be no peace offering from Abel.

After traveling around the country and speaking with various groups, Sadlowski decided to run. Lloyd McBride, the District director in St. Louis, was chosen by Abel to run for president. Sadlowski had little time to build a national organization, and that weakness would show. The campaign organization was named Steelworkers Fight Back when he was running for Director, and for the national campaign, they kept it headquartered in Chicago. Communications with supporters in other districts were poor.

Sadlowski had to employ lawyers to find out where the voters were. The Steelworkers had 1.5 million eligible voters, and the International Union would not give voter information to the Sadlowski campaign. There were 5,500 local unions and 15,000 polling places, but the campaign was not given information about locations. The court orders obtained some information, but it was costly and time-consuming.

The main campaign issue was democracy in the union and the right to ratify the union contracts. This was a good issue in the basic steel locals, where only the local union presidents had a vote when national agreements were negotiated. The average worker was under 30, and there was the most dissatisfaction. The problem was that basic steel had 400,000 members, which was less than one-third of the USW. The rest were in containers: aluminum, chemical, ferrous, and non-ferrous production and fabrication. Most members in other industries and the small shops already had the right to ratify their contracts. So Sadlowski's program did not offer much to those members.

Sadlowski talking with a steelworker.

The campaign was waged across the U.S. and Canada.

Sadlowski talking to steelworkers at a mill.

Sadlowski slate campaign flyer

A popular campaign poster.

Sadlowski used the media in the campaign. He had the look of a steelworker, and reporters loved his background and story. Mike Wallace put him on *60 Minutes,* and he did many magazine and newspaper interviews.

One interview damaged him. An issue of *Penthouse* magazine was published in December 1976, just before the election, featuring an interview with Sadlowski, which hurt his campaign. In the interview, he said he didn't want his children to be steelworkers, and no one should have to work in a steel mill.

From the interview:

Sadlowski: Working 40 hours a week in a steel mill drains the lifeblood of a man. There are workers there right now, full of poems, and doctors who are operating cranes...I advocate putting people who work in steel mills into the medical professions...I never met a steelworker in his right mind who loves what he is doing. No one likes to get up at five in the morning. I remember going to bed at nine o'clock, getting up the next morning, and being so tired I couldn't move. And I have a feeling if such a guy exists, he's some liberal punk who will last two months—and feel like a he-man because he has sweated for once in his life.

The ultimate goal of organized labor is for no man to have to go down to the bowels of the earth and dig coal. No man will have to be subjected to the blast furnace. ***We have reduced the steel labor force from 520,000 fifteen*** *years ago to 400,000 today.* ***Let's reduce them to 100,000.The coal miners went from 400,000 to 68,000***. (emphasis added) *We don't need any more steel mills. We don't need that type of industrial growth at the expense of the environment. We can't consume what existing steel mills produce; let's call a halt. Enough with the car! How many more cars do we need? It's too much. It's gagging me. I like candy, but I get a bellyache. Nothing is to be gained from that. Society has nothing to show for it but waste. How many guys in that mill could be whatever they wanted to be? Whatever the need is – carpet layers, doctors, plumbers – whatever society needs. Let's have the steel industry, by virtue of what it is capable of producing, subsidize education. Do that!*

McBride's team put the interview material in flyers and passed them out at plants. Sadlowski later blamed his comments on drinking, but the damage was done. Marvin Weinstock, who was a candidate for Vice President on Sadlowski's slate, commented at the time, *"In Youngstown, we have strong Sadlowski supporters removing campaign helmet stickers, because they think Ed's for higher unemployment."*

Money was another issue in the campaign. It costs a lot to run a campaign covering the United States and Canada. McBride mainly received his money from union staff who gave requested monthly assessments. Some gave voluntarily, and their Directors pressured some. Sadlowski received the bulk of his money from outside the union.

Sadlowski went to Hollywood to raise money from celebrities, but this allowed McBride to charge that Sadlowski was a captive of the elite. In an op ed, Sadlowski's lawyer, Joseph Rauh, said:

Should non-members be permitted to contribute and otherwise assist in a union election? Abel says no.So do Meany, Shanker, and others. But without public support, the challenger would never have had a chance. Tony Boyle would be president of the UMW today, instead of a lifelong resident of a Pennsylvania prison, if the public had not rallied behind the reform group. The incumbent or his hand-selected candidate has his campaign built in for him.

As the campaign ended, former USW President David McDonald said:

Unless Sadlowski has an overwhelming victory in the U.S., he will not win the presidency. The Canadian return sheets will carry enough votes in favor of Lloyd McBride that he will be declared elected. I know, I stole four elections up there myself.

His statement foretold the result. On February 8, 1977, McBride defeated Sadlowski by nearly 90,000 votes, 338,861 to 249,281. Sadlowski received 52 percent of the votes in locals of 1000 or more—locals that are primarily basic steel mills. He only won 38 percent of the vote in the smaller locals. Sadlowski won majorities in 10 of the union's 25 districts. He needed to win big in the industrial area between Chicago and the East Coast, which had 64 percent of the membership, but he did not. Sadlowski barely broke even in that area. In the three Pittsburgh districts where Narick had gotten 67 percent in 1969, Sadlowski only got 50 percent. In his home district, District 31, he won only 60 percent, which fell short of the nearly 67 percent he had received in the district director election two years earlier.

In Canada, McBride had a 38,000-vote margin. In District 5, which stretches from Quebec to Nova Scotia, the vote was 23,651 for McBride and 2,668 for Sadlowski. McBride also won by about 38,000 votes in the South. So about 85 percent of McBride's margin came from Canada and the South. Sadlowski expected to lose in Canada and the South, where the campaign had no observers, but not by the margin they did. Local unions in the South turned in margins like 49-0, 57-0, 61-0. In Quebec, 59 local unions did not give Sadlowski a single vote. Sadlowski won where he had observers. But in most unions, he had no one.

After the Fight

Steelworkers Fight Back was never really a national organization. It was centered in Chicago, but it did not run candidates for Director in other areas, such as Pittsburgh, Baltimore, Cleveland, and elsewhere. The campaign sent organizers from District 31 to different places, but this meant the vote totals in Sadlowski's home district did not reach the expected level. Sadlowski's win in District 31 did not reach the three-to-one margin the campaign thought was needed to win the election nationally. The campaign put a lot of effort into lawsuits to get local union contact information from the International. This was successful, but building a national rank-and-file organization suffered. This was needed to ensure an accurate vote count in both nations. Canada was a wild card because of a lack of labor laws to enforce fair elections. Also, the McBride team was running a Canadian, Lynn Williams, for Secretary-Treasurer on their ticket, which was a first for the Steelworkers union. This was undoubtedly a source of pride for Canadians.

The campaign left Sadlowski with more than $100,000 in debts ($424,000 in 2025 dollars).He was dispirited, and the **Fight Back** organization dissolved without a charismatic personality to rally around. Sadlowski was appointed as sub-director for the South Chicago area of District 31 of the union. He remained in that position until he retired in 1992. When newly elected District Director Jack Parton re-appointed Sadlowski to the sub-district director position, President Lloyd McBride was furious. He carried on the feud with his old opponent and refused to pay Sadowski the proper salary for the sub-district director job. This would also mean his pension benefits would be lowered. Director Jack Parton was able to argue the point with McBride, and Sadowski got his proper pay and pension benefits from the union. McBride even carried on his feud with Sadlowski's allies. A Steelworker

Fightback supporter, Dave Patterson, was elected to a director position in Canada in 1981. McBride used his influence with the U.S. Border Patrol, causing Patterson to arrive late at several Executive Board meetings in Pittsburgh.

Sadlowski was a big baseball fan, and according to his daughter, Sue Sadlowski Garza, he wanted the job of Director of the Major League Baseball Players Association (MLBPA) more than he wanted to be president of the Steelworkers union. He interviewed for the job when Marvin Miller retired, but was not selected. Miller was on the technical staff of the Steelworkers union when the MLBPA hired him as its first Executive Director. He turned the players' union into the strongest union in professional sports.

At the 1978 International Union Convention, delegates passed a resolution banning outside money in union elections. Pittsburgh did not want another Sadlowski. A lawsuit was filed, and the U.S. Supreme Court accepted the case. In *Steelworkers v. Sadlowski*, 457 U.S. 102 (1982), the court held that the no-outsider rule did not violate the union member's Bill of Rights under the Landrum-Griffin Act.

District 31 Director Jack Parton said:

Sadlowski's campaign brought about significant changes in union finance rules regarding outside funding. Clearly, his campaign was primarily funded by people outside the labor movement. Eddie challenged the rule, and it went all the way to the Supreme Court. You can only use members' money now. I could not get a nickel from my mother if she wanted to help me. Now everything is monitored. Candidates have to file financial reports. There is a downside to restricting campaign contributions to members, but I think the benefits outweigh it. Obviously, it is an advantage to be an incumbent, but that is the case in everything. If you do your god-damned job, you're likely to get reelected.

Victory in Defeat

Although Sadlowski was defeated, the union eventually adopted his main issue—the right to ratify the contract —with the aid of a new Chicago District director. In 1981, Jack Parton, President of Local 1014 at U.S. Steel Gary Works, ran against Jim Balanoff, who had been elected District 31 Director in 1977. Many Sadlowski supporters in the district had grown dissatisfied with Balanoff's management style in union affairs and with his response to the growing layoffs in the district. They used their experience and contact information from the Sadlowski campaign to help get Parton elected. In the election, Parton took six out of the eight sub-districts, losing only Balanoff's home area of Indiana Harbor and a sub-district in the northwest Chicago area. Parton won the district with 52 percent of the vote, 24,289 to 21,708.

McBride died in 1983, and Lynn Williams took over as USW president. Parton and other directors with large numbers of basic steel members urged Williams to give basic steel members the right to ratify their contracts. Parton told Williams that this was the issue that had given Sadlowski the most momentum and that the members deserved the right to vote on their contracts. During this time, steel mills were closing, and 1980 was the last year of contract negotiations with the ENA. The companies withdrew from the agreement and ended industry-coordinated bargaining. Parton said:

I told Lynn Williams, "We have to go to the concept of membership ratification." With the presidents as a group no longer ratifying, it was too much pressure to put on individual presidents. We recommended a process that needed to be put in place and is in place today. Lynn Williams did a lot on the national level to bring people together. He was a visionary.

The International gave members in basic steel the right to vote on their contracts for the first time in 1986. With the collapse of industry-wide bargaining, it would be nearly impossible for the union's Basic Steel Conference to convene to vote on every contract. Lynn Williams also trusted rank-and-file steelworkers far more than past USW presidents. He felt it was their responsibility to endorse the contract they would be working under. The issue that Sadlowski had fought so hard for was adopted almost without dissent with Williams' support.

Before she died, Alice Purela, Local 65 President (US Steel Southworks), a strong Sadlowski supporter, thanked Parton for his support of the right to ratify. She said, "*You gave us something Eddie could not get us – the right to ratify. It is something I never thought I would see.*"

Former Inland Steel Local 1010 President Mike Mezo:

If you ran a campaign like Sadlowski's today, everybody would say, "What the hell are you talking about? Where's the bread and butter?" The mill has been cleaned up. Most of the jobs are not nearly as strenuous or as dirty and nasty. That's why people can work so much overtime now. Compared to the 1970s, you are aristocracy.

Jack Parton

Jack Parton, USWA District 31 (now 7) Director 1981 – 2001.

Jack Parton:

You need good people to discuss where the union is going. It's healthy. We still have debates, but it sends a signal to the companies that they can't divide one group against the other when there is general agreement on big issues. The only thing that stands in the way of corporations just taking all the goddamned money in the country is the labor movement.

Ed Sadlowski:

In the end, I place my faith in the working stiff. He's still the most reliable guy on the street when push comes to shove. There's a sure instinct that a worker has, much more so than some candy-assed store owner. He understands who's screwing him, but he doesn't understand how to get unscrewed. The little Chamber of Commerce storefront man, he never understands he's getting' screwed. He's part of Main Street, America. I firmly believe there is a kid in a shop somewhere who will emerge, rally working people around him, and move the American labor movement in a more militant direction.

Steel Union Insurgency and Other Unions

As Sadowski and Steelworkers Fight Back sought to transform the Steelworkers union, similar movements were at work in other major industrial unions. The United Mine Workers' union had a pro-democracy caucus, Mineworkers For Democracy (MFD). They had organized after a reformer, Joseph Yablonski, was murdered along with his family after contesting the corrupt Tony Boyle for the United Mine Workers presidency in 1969. The MFD successfully gained control of the union in 1972. Some of the MFD campaign veterans worked on the Sadlowski campaign.

Other unions also had rank-and-file groups. In the early 1970s, wildcat strikes broke out in the auto plants. Many of these were a mix of civil rights for black workers and militancy within the union. In Detroit, a group called the Detroit Revolutionary Union Movement led many wildcat strikes in the early 70s. Other plants formed the United National Caucus, which fought the pro-Administration Solidary House for union control. They were not successful but drew support from the United Steelworkers organizing, centered in Chicago. In the Teamsters Union, a group, Teamsters for a Democratic Union, contested the Hoffa regime.

5 New Challenges and New Directions

The 1980s began as the 1970s ended in steel. Companies continued to close mills and departments and to ask for concessions from the union. One case brought national attention when U.S. Steel offered to build a rail mill at the Southworks site in Chicago in April 1981. By this time, employment at Southworks had fallen from a high of 18,000 to 5,000. The mill would require $225 million in investment and bring 1,000 new jobs. But there were conditions. For the rail mill to be built, U.S. Steel had said that the locals must agree to work rules at the mill substantially different from those long in force at South Works and that the state remove a tax on production of rails.

In September, the Illinois Legislature eliminated the rail tax, and the workers agreed, by a 6-to-1 margin, to changes in the way the proposed mill would be staffed, including combining jobs so workers would do a variety of tasks, reducing the need for workers.

But U.S. Steel had already made a third demand: that the Metropolitan Sanitary District ease its requirement that the company spend millions on water pollution controls at its works in nearby Gary, Ind.

"The minute we get this,“ the company chairman, David M. Roderick, said in May 1983, "we'll surge ahead" with the mill's construction.

In August 1983, $30 million earmarked for pollution controls in Gary became available to the mill.

But more than two years had passed since the mill was proposed. Railroads had merged. Thousands of miles of track were closing. Imported rails had seized some 15 percent of the American market. Meanwhile, U.S. Steel continued to experience deep losses, and construction costs of the mill had soared. Construction was delayed.

In March 1983, the major American steelmakers, including U.S. Steel, won concessions amounting to more than $1 billion over a 41-month national contract.

In November, Thomas C. Graham, U.S. Steel's vice chairman and chief operating officer, said that, because of "new realities," the company needed concessions throughout South Works, not just in the proposed rail mill. It called for extensive subcontracting, a combination of jobs, and reductions in overtime and benefits totaling about $1.40 an hour. If the local agreed, Mr. Graham said, “We can begin work on the rail mill in 90 days."

The new demands aroused a furor in the local community. On Dec. 11, 1983, the national union leadership said locals could not agree to any concessions that would alter the national agreement. Many top union leaders believed U.S. Steel and other producers were playing one local against another. Ten days later, workers rejected the demands. On Dec. 27, U.S. Steel canceled the rail mill.

This dispute poisoned relations between the top steelmaker and the union. The union sued in court for breach of contract, but in early 1986, a jury ruled that U.S. Steel was not liable.

The Longest Lockout in USW History

1986 lockout by USX (U.S. Steel).

The 1980s were a bloodbath for the steel industry as it struggled to survive. Steel prices were falling as new mills came online worldwide. The trends that had started in the 1960s and 1970s – the importation of steel and the substitution of plastics and aluminum for steel – accelerated in the 1980s. In 1974, there were 610,000 people employed in the U.S. steel industry. By 1984, it was down to 236,000. It dropped further to 125,600 in 1994. The sector underwent bankruptcies and consolidation.

The union tried to survive as it faced these challenges. As members dropped, it was forced to cut services and lay off staff.

In 1986, at U.S. Steel (now renamed USX after it bought two oil producers), relations between the company and the union were at a low. No one trusted what either side said. U.S. Steel had gone from a company with 80,000 employees in 1980 to 22,100 working union employees in 1986. The company wanted to contract out jobs to save money, and the union wanted to keep as many jobs as possible. The contract was due to expire on August 1st, and negotiations were at a standstill. The union had given many of USX's competitors concession contracts since they were in or facing bankruptcy. The day before, the union offered to continue working, but the company claimed it was just a ruse to claim unemployment benefits in the event of a strike. The company said the union had effectively called a strike, and they locked the union out.

This labor stoppage (lockout) was the longest in USW history, lasting six months from August 1, 1986, to January 31, 1987. The 22,000 strikers were able to collect unemployment benefits in all seven states where USX had mills, except in Illinois. In Illinois, a state law denied benefits regardless of whether a stoppage was a strike or a lockout.

District director Jack Parton said:

We were worried about unemployment benefits in Indiana since it had a Republican governor. But Lew Johnson at our office had gotten a $1 million grant from the state for dislocated workers a couple of years before. The state was happy with the results, and the governor approved our unemployment benefits.

Before this round of bargaining, we engaged in pattern bargaining with all the steel companies. There were 10 nationwide, and by this time, about seven remained, although LTV Steel was near bankruptcy. USX led the bargaining for all the companies, and the rest of them would accept whatever they agreed to. In past contracts, USX agreed to things they knew other competitors could not afford in an attempt to drive them out of business.

This time, USX dropped out of the pattern bargaining and said they were going at it alone. I was chair of the Inland negotiations. We first got an agreement with Bethlehem, which was the strongest. LTV declared bankruptcy in July and cut off health benefits for retirees. I ordered the union to strike at Indiana Harbor, and they were out on a wildcat for five days. A judge restored the health benefits because the LTV creditors feared losing orders.

At the USX plant, protection personnel told us the company had ordered a bunch of small arms. They went to the sheriffs of Lake and Porter Counties to get their help in enforcing order on the picket lines. Both sheriffs told them they would not go against the Steelworkers.

Management employees had been loading trucks and trains with previously produced steel that had been kept in inventory and were trying to ship it to customers. We had a rally in Gary, and we could have gone into the plant and stopped the shipments, but some religious leaders stopped us from doing so, so they could pray. The union was giving out $60 a week to those who could show need. This led to disputes at the local level.

By January 1987, USX was about to lose major orders for car manufacturers, and union members were running out of unemployment benefits. The dispute was settled, with the union receiving restrictions on subcontracting and the company receiving wage concessions. The vote to accept a new contract was 19,621 in favor and 4045 against. The contract included early-retirement incentives and eliminated 1,300 union jobs. A few days after the lockout ended, USX announced four of its mills would be permanently closed, eliminating 3,500 jobs.

New Directions in Work and in Bargaining

The USW was hemorrhaging members. In 1988, the union had about half the members it had at the beginning of the decade. Attempts to recruit new members resulted in few numbers, even when successful. New companies did not fit into the mold of traditional union employers. In the heyday of union organization, hundreds of workers lived near their workplaces and shared common interests specific to a single employer or industry. In the latter part of the twentieth century, the decline of large industry and the mobility of the workforce meant organizing was far more difficult. Workers are scattered and firms are small. One USW leader expressed his frustration: "We organized '*three or four plants, each with thirty workers, and then a single department of a steel mill closes, costing us 500 members.*"

In the midst of this turbulent decade, the union and companies began experimenting with ways to both save jobs and save money. One of the experiments was the Labor Management Participation Teams (LMPT).There were successes with these teams here and there, but at the plant level, neither the union nor management really bought into them. According to Sam Camens, a USW official in charge of participation efforts, the teams took up a broad range of subjects. He said 2 percent dealt strictly with employee concerns, such as food machines and locker room facilities; 7 percent with labor relations; 5 percent with scheduling; and 84 percent with quality, production, and maintenance. Camens told Congress that the teams developed a tool and a parts-availability program for a blast furnace, which cost $16,000 and saved $330,000 a year in furnace delays. Changes were made to the hot-bed operation of a rolling mill (where steel bars are placed for cooling) to eliminate bends in steel billets. The savings totaled millions of dollars. A third project involved developing standards to eliminate excess rolling (production) for each order in a department, resulting in savings of over $700,000.

Nevertheless, this experiment faded. Some companies have never tried the teams. Others tried them, but just did it in one or two areas instead of throughout the plant.This meant that whenever there was a problem, it was easy for management, the union, or both to retreat into the safe space of how things had always been done.

At the Chicago district of LTV Steel, LMPT faced several problems that it would face elsewhere. LMPT was instituted during a period of layoffs, a financial crisis, and restructuring. People associate a new program with all the turmoil occurring around them in those situations. A company can't wait for an economic crisis to end before attempting change. Management and labor representatives must try to show that participation relationships will be a way out of a situation, not a function of it.

When participation teams are restricted, as in LMPT agreements, so that they can't discuss matters that may be the subject of contract complaints, there is always a potential for abuse. If a union representative does not want a team to discuss something, all the rep has to do is file a complaint about it. This should not be a limitation for teams; otherwise, their work can be held hostage. If a team can't make changes to a local agreement, it faces unacceptable restrictions on introducing innovation. There can be guidance on these matters from a plant union/company committee, but there should be no hard-and-fast rules.

Local union politics, combined with management's unwillingness to meet this head-on, killed off LMPT in LTV Chicago. One way to solve this problem is to take the responsibility for LMPT operations out of the local union and management. Other companies have tried to make participation in the teams part of the national contract.

Experiments in Local Mill Manning

There have been constant disputes between the steel companies and the union over work rules. This has led companies to use contractors to perform some of the work that union members usually do. At the Chicago Republic Steel plant, Local 1033 faced two related issues as the 1980s began. Craft members from the central shops were being laid off as the mill contracted. The company began using contractors to do some of the work previously done by the crafts. This was a contract violation, but grievances must be filed by someone who witnessed it. Not all violations are seen, or if seen, reported. If a grievance is filed, it may take months or longer to be settled. In the meantime, craft members remained laid off.

Pete O'Day, Boilermaker, Local 1033 Grievance Committeeman for the centralized crafts:

"For the first time, the skilled tradesmen of the centralized craft shops (riggers, carpenters, boilermakers, machinists, welders, pipefitters, and motor repairmen) were being laid off in large numbers. The company was using contractors to perform the work of these members in violation of the contract. The union was filing grievances when it could, but the restitution process was lengthy and proving not to be costly enough to inhibit the company's actions. In addition to the problem of contracting out their work, these craftsmen's duties were also being assigned to various department's millwrights on a piecemeal basis by the company (a hours' worth of welding here, and hours' worth of pipefitting there) – thus in effect the company was using millwrights as forced 'generalized craftsmen', wherever they could, and without negotiations with the union, and supplementing this piecemeal cross-craft work theft with full time outside contractors where the work scope demanded greater skill and experience unique to one of the crafts. This situation was not tolerable. The central crafts were the backbone of the union because, unlike millwrights and production workers whose permanent work assignment was to a single location and process, the central crafts traveled throughout the plant on a daily basis, applying their skills in maintenance and construction everywhere and interacting with and getting to know all of the 5,000 members of the local union. The crafts were very active union supporters, and, generally speaking, were older and had much more seniority than

the department millwrights, who continued to work while the craft members were laid off.

The union had to face the reality that its attempt thus far to defend its jurisdiction over the type of skilled work being performed, and by whom, was not succeeding. The company had, in effect, imposed multicraft work without considering plant seniority. The union had to have plant seniority, which was a core union principle.

The local union's goal thus shifted from defending the lost cause of maintaining craft jurisdiction rules – governing which skilled union members performed what work -- to defending the foundational principle that seniority determined who did and did not get laid off and called back to work. The union's goal in the multicraft negotiations then became the defense of seniority and the defense of the right of the union to have its members perform all normal skilled and production work based solely on seniority, and to stop the contracting out. The capricious actions of the company to favor certain younger or more favored employees had to end. The local also sought to defend the apprenticeship program, because, if there was going to be a new job that was in effect a "general multi-craft mechanic," it was going to come from a negotiated agreement, with the job duties would be the same for all, and all would be professionally trained.

We had no playbook for this. We were leading the union in the field of multicraft. We had representatives of every craft discuss what was needed. If we were going to have layoffs, we wanted them to be as fair as possible. The company wanted relaxation of work rules. So we had leverage. The company gave us early retirement pensions with an extra $400 a month, which eased the layoffs.

When the General Mechanic Agreement was put to a vote, all crafts and millwrights were entitled to vote, including those on layoff. The vote was 265 Yes and 89 No. When the agreement went into effect, 263 craft members came back to work, and 263 millwrights were laid off. The layoffs were lessened by the number of those going on early retirement pensions.

Did it work? Unfortunately, the economic trends continued. Several departments of the mill shut down over the next few years. We had hoped for the transfer of work from Ohio to Chicago. That did not happen. There were 624 central craft members in 1982 and fewer than 50 by 1988. There was temporary success in jobs where people could be cross-trained quickly. Those jobs that required extensive training were not completed due to the economic downturn."

Victor Storino, Rigger, Local 1033 President from 1988 until the mill shut down in 2002, and former Grievance Committeeman for the crafts:

The big problem was the contractors. We did not know the specialized contractors. We attended training at Indiana University Northwest in Gary, but it wasn't clear what the contractors knew about a special piece of equipment. As the plant entered an economic downturn, the training was canceled. The company wanted to cut the force by about one-half. At the end, contractors came in.

The company became an employee-owned company (ESOP), but it kept the old management. In the first year, the on-time delivery rate was 98%. Then the company said there were too many supervisors. They cut 20% of the supervisors, and the on-time delivery rate dropped to 85%. They should have listened to the employees, but they said they would not let the employees run the mill.

Jerry Novak, Welder and Grievance Committeeman for the 14” Bar Mill:

After the General Mechanic position was created, the company never eliminated the central shops. This led to resentments between those assigned to departments and those assigned to the central shops. (Novak was eventually laid off and hired by a railroad.)The Steelworkers were a far stronger union than the railroads' unions. In the railroad industry, all occupations are split into separate unions for pipefitters, boilermakers, electricians, and others. The steel mills just had one union, and it was much better.

The Combination of Work and Education

UNITED STEELWORKERS

ICD

PARTICIPATING COMPANIES

The Chicago-area district of the Steelworkers, District 31 (now 7), created an innovative career education program that has spread nationwide. Together with 12 participating companies, the union made the Institute for Career Development (ICD). Its main headquarters is in Merrillville, Indiana, but it now has teaching centers at 50 steel centers across the country.

ICD teaching center in New Carlisle, Indiana

Employees can sign up for about 1,000 courses.Title examples include: Buying Rental Properties, Laser

Engraving, Easy Guitar, Kybex Holster Creation, Tariffs, Stock Markets, Private Pilot Ground School, and CDL Tractor Trailer. The Institute is funded by a contribution from the 12 participating companies of 15 cents an hour for each hour a USW employee works. These courses not only can educate an employee about hobbies or outside interests, but also can provide the education needed to allow them to bid on higher jobs at the steel mill.

ICD is not only a great benefit but a motivational tool in the quest for a better life for all.

David McCall, President of the USW

Roxanne Brown, Incoming President March 2026

New Directions in Bargaining

Lynn R. Williams 1924 – 2014.

USW President Lynn Williams, in his final term, wanted to change the bargaining culture of the union and the steel companies. He said:

We wanted an industry that was composed of profitable, productive, successful enterprises that paid decent wages and provided good benefits. We wanted employment security for steelworkers. We did not want our people and their communities' jobs given away to contractors. We wanted an industry in which our people had a significant voice —not simply on shop-floor improvements, though they were important —but at every level of the industry, including the boardroom. We wanted more training, particularly in the trades areas, so that more of our people could aspire to be tradespersons. We wanted a more sweeping policy of joint union-industry approaches to government in pursuit of a more vigorous pro-steel policy in areas of trade and other subjects in which we agreed.

Williams called this approach New Directions. It had two core principles. The first is that one has a greater stake in the ongoing success of an enterprise than its workers do. The second was that the best way to achieve that success was to involve the workers and their union in the management and decision-making processes —not superficially, but in real and meaningful ways. These principles involved broad-ranging new proposals, the most significant of which were employment-security guarantees and partnership agreements, providing for union and worker involvement at every level from the board of directors to the plant floor.

The USW Basic Steel Conference adopted the policy and agreed to present the following points in bargaining:

- Adoption of an employment security (no layoffs) program based on the National Steel model.
- Union and worker involvement at all levels, from the shop floor to the boardroom. At upper management levels, it includes participation in the development of the business plan as it deals with products, markets, capital spending, and in decisions involving technological change. Finally, it means access to all information necessary to perform the participatory roles.
- Long-term agreements are considered only if they include re-openers with experimental negotiating agreement-type arbitration and other upside protection should the company prosper during the agreement.
- Restructuring the way work is done in the workplace to reduce costs and make the workplace less authoritarian, safer, fairer, and rewarding in terms of worker skills and involvement in the solution of operating problems.

- Health-care cost reductions through managed-care alternatives. Plans on a single company or multi-company basis.

- Funding of retiree health care and other legacy costs by the company and through other means as well.

- Additional corporatc and successorship guarantees to make sure the entire corporate entity and its assets stand behind benefit obligations, notwithstanding sales and corporate maneuvers.

- Revitalized apprenticeship and training programs in which the parties jointly determine the manpower needs in the craft occupations and how to fill them.

- Company neutrality in organizing campaigns and recognition of the union once we achieve a majority status through signed authorization cards.

- Investment commitments.

- Elimination of all significant remaining contracting-out problems.

- Development of a joint public policy and legislative agenda, including labor law reform, health care, trade, legacy costs, and a steel tripartite commission.

In the ensuing negotiations, most objectives were achieved, with certain company-specific exceptions. U.S. Steel did not want anyone on its board, but the union nominated former Secretary of Labor Ray Marshall. The company not only accepted him but waived its mandatory retirement age so Marshall could continue to serve.

New Directions was a big leap for the conservative steel industry and for some reluctant union officials. President Williams said:

New Directions was an exciting, unprecedented attempt to move an entire industry toward new, participatory ideas about the organization of work and the role of workers in it. And the attempt was made in one of the oldest, most conservative industries at a time when it could almost be considered under siege. It was a bigger leap forward than many managers and a number of our people were comfortable with; they felt that if the old ways were working tolerably well, they should be left alone. On the other hand, when people on both sides were interested, they could accomplish great things. I learned over and over again that changing the culture of the union, or the companies, or of both together was no simple task.

New Directions forever changed the industry. Hundreds of employees had more confidence in their own abilities and understanding, less false respect for supervisors who did not deserve any, and much greater respect for those who did. The end result is that the dreams of the Steelworkers' founder, Philip Murray, regarding industrial democracy are closer to realization today than ever before. There are people in all the shops who have a fundamental understanding of how things work and of what a significant contribution they can make. Knowledge is power, a slogan Murray would undoubtedly have appreciated. It is in abundance these days.

Continuing Obstacles

As the years of the new century pass, the union is facing many of the same problems as before. U.S. Steel had continued to close older mills. Nippon Steel agreed to buy U.S. Steel in late 2023. This made Nippon Steel the second-largest steel manufacturer in the world.

There was immediate opposition from union and political leaders due to foreign ownership of an icon of American industry. Concerns were raised about union contracts, supply chains, and national security. Supporters argued that Nippon had agreed to invest two billion dollars in older mills in Gary and the Pittsburgh area. The deal became embroiled in the 2024 election, with President Biden (and then VP Harris) saying it should be blocked. Former President Trump, running for re-election, also said he would block the deal. Local unions in Gary and Pittsburgh backed the deal, breaking with the International Union leadership. Local mayors in Gary and the Pittsburgh area also backed the deal.

After Trump became president again, he spoke with local union leaders and agreed to let the deal go through, with a provision for a 'Golden Share'. This share meant the U.S. government would effectively control much of U.S. Steel's operations. After the deal was finalized, U.S. Steel attempted to close its Granite Steel mill in Illinois. Trump exercised the golden share and told them the operation must continue and that the workers must be retained.

The Future of the USW Union

What began as a union of mostly steelworkers in 1942 continues to transform itself and its membership into a diverse coalition of workers from virtually every segment of the economy. Over the past 78 years, the USW has merged with the International Union of Mine, Mill and Smelter Workers; the United Stone and Allied Products Workers of America; the Upholsterers International Union; the United Rubber Workers; the Aluminum, Brick & Glass Workers; the Industrial Wood and Allied Workers of Canada and the Paper, Allied-Industrial, Chemical and Energy Workers Union, among others.

As former USW President Leo Gerard said:

The USW has mobilized members, other unions, and the public to support the Occupational and Health Act, the Clean Air Act, the Civil Rights Act, the Voting Rights Act, Pension reform (ERISA), and the many subsequent victories that have improved the quality of life for citizens across North America. Through the 1970s and '80s, as an energy crisis, trade imbalance, and economic recession threatened the survival of the domestic steel industry and jobs for thousands of steelworkers, mergers, organizing, and coalition-building became even more critical for the USW. None of these achievements would have been possible without the USW and their allies taking to the streets, to their Capitol halls, and to their legislators' offices with a clear message: We are one.

Though the future undoubtedly depends on more partnerships like these, there is at least one thing that has not changed in all these years: members are the ones who hold that future in their hands. Organizing and energizing new members and workplaces, tapping the vast knowledge and experience of longtime members, and joining forces across any barrier that divides us with all those who share our mission are all essential to the future of a union that never stops moving forward.

UNITED STEELWORKERS
USW™

Appendix A

A Timeline of Steelworker History

August 4, 1876 Amalgamated Association of Iron and Steel Workers (AA) was formed.

July 1, 1892 Homestead Works strike began.

August 1, 1901 U.S. Steel union recognition strike fails.

September 22, 1919 Great Steel Strike begins.

November 9, 1935 Committee on Industrial Organizations was formed.

June 7, 1936 Steel Worker Organizing Committee (SWOC) was created.

March 7, 1937 First SWOC contract signed with US Steel. This was followed by the 'Little Steel' independent companies in 1941-1942.

May 30, 1937 Chicago, Memorial Day Massacre.

May 22, 1942 United Steelworkers (USWA) union was formed. Philip Murray was appointed president.

June, 1944 Aluminum Workers of America merged with the USWA.

February 13, 1945 First USWA election. Philip Murray was elected as well as the initial Directors.

January, 1946 First of five post-WWII strikes by the USWA for wage increases.

October 31, 1949 First agreement for company-funded pension plan with Bethlehem Steel.

November, 1952 Philip Murray dies. David McDonald appointed USWA President.

1955 The USWA reaches one million members.

July 1, 1959 Beginning of the 116-day strike against the steel industry. Largest in U.S. history. Results in cost-of-living wage protection, but also leads to an increase in imported steel.

February, 1965 I.W. Abel was elected USWA President in a close election with McDonald.

August, 1968 Creation of a strike and defense fund.

December 20, 1970 Occupational Health and Safety Administration (OSHA) was passed into law. USWA promoted the law.

June 1972, expedited arbitration was created in Basic Steel. One thousand cases are settled in two and a half years.

March, 1973 Experimental Negotiating Agreement in Basic Steel

April, 1974 Consent Decree was court-ordered for the major steel companies and the USWA.

September, 1974 Pension Reform (ERISA) was signed into law. ERISA was promoted by USW.

February 8, 1977 Lloyd McBride was elected USWA President, defeating Chicagoan Ed Sadlowski.

March 29, 1984 Lynn Williams becomes USWA President.

July 1, 1986, Lockout began at U.S. Steel. Lasts Six Months. This is the longest labor dispute with a Basic steel company in USW history.

March, 1993 USW adopts New Directions Bargaining.

November, 1993 George Becker was elected USWA President.

February, 2001, Leo Gerard was elected USWA President.

March, 2004 End of a seven-year company lockout at Oregon Steel. This was the longest labor dispute in USWA history. One hundred million dollars in back pay was awarded.

April, 2005 The USWA and the Paper, Chemical, and Energy workers merge, becoming the largest industrial union in the U.S. The union changes its name to the USW.

July, 2019 Thomas Conroy becomes USW President.

October, 2023 David McCall becomes USW President.

Appendix B

Documents in Steel Labor History

APPENDIX B – 1

REPUBLIC STEEL'S EFFORT TO OPPOSE ORGANIZING

(Republic Steel sent this letter to all of its employees in July 1936)

To Our Employees:

We are making the following statement so you will know the attitude of the Republic toward the recently announced campaign for unionization of the steelworkers.

The leader of this drive is John L. Lewis, head of the Coal Miners' Union. He is not connected with the steel industry. Representatives of radical and communist groups are helping in this movement. William Z. Foster, chairman of the Communist Party, has announced his support. Foster was the leader of the unsuccessful attempt to unionize the steel industry in 1919.

What Do They Want? John L. Lewis and his organization want more workers to pay them dues. If they could organize the steel workers, they hope to collect $5,000,000 a year from them. Republic employees alone would pay over half a million dollars. Furthermore, they could place dues and assessments at any figure they liked, and the steelworkers would have to pay them.

The real aim of the present organization drive is to establish a closed shop. They want to force you into the union and make you pay for the right to work. Under a "Closed Shop," every man has to pay his dues to the union whether he wants to or not. If he gets behind in dues, they can throw him out of the union. By this threat, they can keep the dues rolling in.

One of the announced purposes of this drive is to throw out your Employee Representation Plan, which you elected, for collective bargaining with the management. The union wants to destroy all Employee Representation Plans in the steel industry.

Your Employee Representation Plan is not run by outsiders. It works. Under your plan, you select your own Employee Representatives – men you know and with whom you work. Under a union, you would be represented by outsiders who may know little or nothing about your problems, your management, or the steel industry. Furthermore, you would have no choice in their selection. You would have to pay money to be dictated to by somebody you did not even know.

What Are Their Methods? The methods customarily used by professional union agitators and organizers are force, coercion, and intimidation of workers and their families. They threaten to call a strike to force men to join their union. They try to force mills to stop operation and keep men from their work for months at a time. They do this to scare men into their union who they know do not want to join the union.

What is the Republic's Stand? Republic stands for the open shop principle. No employee has to join any organization to get or hold a job. Advancement depends on individual merit and effort.

The Republic will not permit any activities within its plant that will interfere with the orderly conduct of operations, stir up strife or discontent, and threaten the peace and comfort of its workers and their families.

Every Republic employee owes a duty of loyalty to the Company so that its best interests may be served. Conduct detrimental to the interests of the Company and which may disrupt the satisfactory relations between employees and management will not be tolerated.

APPENDIX B - 2

First Contract Agreement Achieved by SWOC

This contract was between the Steel Workers Organizing Committee and Carnegie-Illinois Steel, which was part of U.S. Steel, and was agreed to on March 2, 1937.

This Agreement, dated March 17, 1937 between Carnegie-Illinois Steel Corporation (hereinafter referred to as the "Corporation") and the Steel Workers Organizing Committee on behalf of the members of the Amalgamated Association of Iron, Steel and Tin Workers of North America, or its successor, (hereinafter referred to as the "Union") employed by the Corporation, made pursuant to and in supplement of Section 4 of the Agreement of March 2, 1937, between said parties.

Section 1.It is the intent and purpose of the parties hereto that this Agreement will promote and improve industrial and economic relationships between those employees who are members of the Union and the Corporation, and to set forth herein the basic Agreement covering rates of pay, hours of work, and conditions of employment to be observed between the parties hereto.

It is understood and agreed that this Agreement pertains only to members of the Union employed in the corporation's steel manufacturing and by-product coke products.

The term "employee", as used in this Agreement, shall not include Foreman, Assistant Foreman, or Supervisors in charge of any classes of labor, or Watchmen, or any salaried employees.

Section 2 – Recognition. The Corporation recognizes the Union as the collective bargaining agency for those employees of the Corporation who are members of the Union. The Corporation recognizes and will not interfere with the right of its employees to become members of the Union. There shall be no discrimination, interference, restraint, or coercion by the Corporation or any of its agents against the members because of membership in the Union. The Union agrees not to intimidate or coerce employees into membership and also not to solicit membership on Corporation time or plant property.

Section 3 – Wages. Effective March 16, 1937, there shall be an increase in wages of ten cents an hour on all rates which are at present Four Dollars and twenty cents ($4.20) a day, or a minimum for this classification of Five Dollars ($5.00) a day of eight (8) hours. Such classifications now receiving less than Four Dollars and twenty cents ($4.20) a day or less than fifty-two and one-half cents per hour shall be increased ten cents per hour. There shall be an increase of ten cents per hour in all other hourly rates, and an equivalent increase in all tonnage and piece-work rates (which will not under normal expected earning [an] increase) of not less than eighty cents per day of eight (8) hours.

Section 4 – Hours of Work. Effective March 16, 1937, there shall be established an eight (8) hour day and a forty (40) hour week. Time and one-half shall be paid for all overtime in excess of eight (8) hours in any one day or for all overtime in excess of forty (40) hours in one week.

A day may be a calendar day or any 24-hour period, and a week may be a calendar week or any five (5) regular 8-hour turns on consecutive days, followed by a 48-hour rest period, at the option of the Corporation.

An employee, who is a member of the Union, shall not be paid both daily and weekly overtime for the same hours worked.

Section 5 – Vacations. Each employee who is a member of the Union and who (prior to July 1, 1937) was continually in the service of the Corporation five (5) years or more (continuity of service to be based on United States Steel and Carnegie Pension Fund rules for Service continuity) shall receive one week's vacation with pay, such vacation to be taken in a single period. Those who are granted vacations will be paid on their average rate of earnings per hour for the two pay periods immediately preceding their vacation. The total hours of vacation pay will be the average hours they worked per week during that period, but not less than 40 hours, nor more than 48 hours.

Vacations will, so far as possible, be granted at times most desired by employees, but the final right to allotment of the vacation period is exclusively reserved to the Corporation to ensure the orderly operation of the Plants.

Section 6 – Seniority. It is understood and agreed that in all cases of promotion and increase or decrease of forces, the following factors shall be considered, and where factors (b), (c), (d), and (e) are relatively equal, length of continuous service shall govern.

(a)Length of continuous service.

(b)Knowledge, training, ability, skill, and efficiency.

(c)Physical fitness.

(d)Family status; number of dependents, etc.

(e)Place of residence.

Section 7 – Adjustment of Grievances. Should differences arise between the corporation and the Union or its members employed by the Corporation as to the meaning and application of the provisions of this Agreement, or should any local trouble of any kind arise in any plant, there shall be no suspension of work on account of such differences, but an earnest effort shall be made to settle such difference immediately in the following manner:

First, between the aggrieved employee, who is a member of the Union, and the Foreman of the department involved.

Second, between a member or members of the Grievance Committee, designated by the Union, and the Foreman and Superintendent of the Department.

Third, between a member or members of the Grievance Committee, designated by the Union, and the General Superintendent or Manager of the Plant.

Fourth, between the Representatives of the National organization of the Union and the Representatives of the Executives of the Corporation.

Fifth, in the event the dispute shall not have been satisfactorily settled, the matter shall then be appealed to an impartial umpire to be appointed by mutual agreement of the parties hereto. The decision of the umpire shall be final. The expense and salary incident to the services of the umpire shall be paid jointly by the Corporation and the Union.

Specified periods shall be agreed upon between the Grievance Committee and the General Superintendent or Manager of each plant for the presentation of grievances hereunder; provided, however, that matters pertaining to discharge (or other matters that cannot reasonably be delayed until the time of the next regular meeting) may be presented at any time in accordance with the foregoing provisions.

The Grievance Committee for each plant shall consist of not less than three employees of that plant, and not more than ten (10) such employees, designated by the Union, who will be afforded such time off, without pay, as may be required:

First, to attend regularly scheduled committee meetings,

Second, to attend meetings pertaining to discharges or other matters which cannot reasonably be delayed until the time of the next regular meeting, and

Third, any member of the Grievance Committee shall have the right to visit departments other than his own at all reasonable times for the purpose of transacting the legitimate business of the Grievance Committee, after notice to and permission from his department superintendent or his designated representative.

The actual number of members of the Grievance Committee at each plant shall be mutually agreed upon between the General Superintendent or Manager of the Plant and the Union, and in no case shall there be more than one member in any department.

Section 8 – Management. The management of the works and the direction of the working forces, including the right to hire, suspend or discharge for proper cause, or transfer, and the right to relive employees from duty because of lack of work, or for some legitimate reasons, is vested exclusively in the Corporation, provided that this will not be used for the purposes of discrimination against any member of the Union.

Section 9 – Discharge Cases. In the event a member of the Union shall be discharged from his employment from and after the date hereof, and he believes he has been unjustly dealt with, such discharge shall constitute a case arising under the method of adjusting grievances herein provided. In the event it should be decided under the rules of this Agreement that an injustice has been dealt the employee with regard to the discharge, the Corporation shall reinstate such employee and pay full compensation at the employee's regular rate of pay for the time lost. All such cases of discharge shall be taken up and disposed of within five (5) days from the date of the discharge.

Section 10 – Safety and Health. The Corporation shall continue to make reasonable provisions for the safety and health of its employees at the plant during the hours of their employment. Protective devices, wearing apparel, and other equipment necessary to properly protect employees from injury shall be provided by the Corporation in accordance with the practice now prevailing in each separate plant. Proper heating and ventilating systems shall be installed where needed.

Section 11 – Individual Wage Rates. Where alleged inequalities in wage rates prevail, the matter may be taken up for local plant adjustment and settlement made on a mutually satisfactory basis.

Section 12 – Future Conferences. Joint conferences between Representatives of the Corporation and of the Union shall commence in Pittsburgh, Pa., on February 7, 1938, for the purpose of negotiating an Agreement with regard to wages, hours, and working conditions, to take effect upon the expiration of this Agreement.

Section 13 – Holidays. The following days shall be considered Holidays, during which there shall be no regular production work, except in cases of continuous operations, on July 4th, Labor Day, and Christmas.

Section 14 – Termination Date. This agreement shall remain in full force and effect until February 28, 1938, inclusive.

CARNEGIE-ILLINOIS STEEL CORPORATION

By B.F. Fairless, President

STEEL WORKERS ORGANIZING COMMITTEE

By Philip Murray, Chairman

APPENDIX B-3

Union members' bill of rights

LANDRUM-GRIFFIN ACT (29 U.S.C. 411)

The Labor-Management Reporting and Disclosure Act (LMRDA) — also known as the Landrum-Griffin Act — deals with the relationship between a union and its members. The LMRDA grants certain rights to union members and protects their interests by promoting democratic procedures within labor organizations. The Act establishes a Bill of Rights for union members; reporting requirements for labor organizations, union officers and employees, employers, labor-relations consultants, and surety companies; standards for the regular election of union officers; and safeguards for protecting labor organization funds and assets.

The Secretary of Labor enforces certain provisions of the LMRDA and has delegated that authority to the Office of Labor-Management Standards (OLMS) of the Department of Labor's Employment Standards Administration.

TITLE I — BILL OF RIGHTS OF MEMBERS OF LABOR ORGANIZATIONS

SEC. 101. (a)(1) EQUAL RIGHTS. — Every member of a labor organization shall have equal rights and privileges within such organization to nominate candidates, to vote in elections or referendums of the labor organization, to attend membership meetings, and to participate in the deliberations and voting upon the business of such meetings, subject to reasonable rules and regulations in such organization's constitution and bylaws.

(2) FREEDOM OF SPEECH AND ASSEMBLY. — Every member of any labor organization shall have the right to meet and assemble freely with other members; and to express any views, arguments, or opinions; and to express at meetings of the labor organization his views, upon candidates in an election of the labor organization or upon any business properly before the meeting, subject to the organization's established and reasonable rules pertaining to the conduct of meetings: Provided, That nothing herein shall be construed to impair the right of a labor organization to adopt and enforce reasonable rules as to the responsibility of every member toward the organization as an institution and to his refraining from conduct that would interfere with its performance of its legal or contractual obligations.

(3) DUES, INITIATION FEES, AND ASSESSMENTS. — Except in the case of a federation of national or international labor organizations, the rates of dues and initiation fees payable by members of any labor organization in effect on the date of enactment of this Act shall not be increased, and no general or special assessment shall be levied upon such members, except-

(A) in the case of a local organization, (i) by majority vote by secret ballot of the members in good standing voting at a general or special membership meeting, after reasonable notice of the intention to vote upon such question, or (ii) by majority vote of the members in good standing voting in a membership referendum conducted by secret ballot; or

(B) in the case of a labor organization, other than a local labor organization or a federation of national or international labor organizations, (i) by majority vote of the delegates voting at a regular convention, or at a special convention of such labor organization held upon not less than thirty days' written notice to the principal office of each local or constituent labor organization entitled to such notice, or (ii) by majority vote of the members in good standing of such labor organization voting in a membership referendum conducted by secret ballot, or (iii) by majority vote of the members of the executive board or similar governing body of such labor organization, pursuant to express authority contained in the constitution and bylaws of such labor organization: Provided, That such action on the part of the executive board or similar governing body shall be effective only until the next regular convention of such labor organization.

(4) PROTECTION OF THE RIGHT TO SUE. — No labor organization shall limit the right of any member thereof to institute an action in any court, or in a

proceeding before any administrative agency, irrespective of whether or not the labor organization or its officers are named as defendants or respondents in such action or proceeding, or the right of any member of a labor organization to appear as a witness in any judicial, administrative, or legislative proceeding, or to petition any legislature or to communicate with any legislator: Provided, That any such member may be required to exhaust reasonable hearing procedures (but not to exceed a four-month lapse of time) within such organization, before instituting legal or administrative proceedings against such organizations or any officer thereof: And provided further, That no interested employer or employer association shall directly or indirectly finance, encourage, or participate in, except as a party, any such action, proceeding, appearance, or petition.

(5) SAFEGUARDS AGAINST IMPROPER DISCIPLINARY ACTION. — No member of any labor organization may be fined, suspended, expelled, or otherwise disciplined except for nonpayment of dues by such organization or by any officer thereof unless such member has been (A) served with written specific charges; (B) given a reasonable time to prepare his defense; (C) afforded a full and fair hearing.

(b) Any provision of the constitution and bylaws of any labor organization which is inconsistent with the provisions of this section shall be of no force or effect.

Civil Enforcement

(29 U.S.C. 412)

SEC. 102. Any person whose rights secured by the provisions of this title have been infringed by any violation of this title may bring a civil action in a district court of the United States for such relief (including injunctions) as may be appropriate. Any such action against a labor organization shall be brought in the district court of the United States for the district where the alleged violation occurred, or where the principal office of such labor organization is located.

Retention of Existing Rights

(29 U.S.C. 413)

SEC. 103. Nothing contained in this title shall limit the rights and remedies of any member of a labor organization under any State or Federal law or before any court or other tribunal, or under the constitution and bylaws of any labor organization.

Right to Copies of Collective Bargaining Agreements

(29 U.S.C. 414)

SEC. 104. It shall be the duty of the secretary or corresponding principal officer of each labor organization, in the case of a local labor organization, to forward a copy of each collective bargaining agreement made by such labor organization with any employer to any employee who requests such a copy and whose rights as such employee are directly affected by such agreement, and in the case of a labor organization other than a local labor organization, to forward a copy of any such agreement to each constituent unit which has members directly affected by such agreement; and such officer shall maintain at the principal office of the labor organization of which he is an officer copies of any such agreement made or received by such labor organization, which copies shall be available for inspection by any member or by any employee whose rights are affected by such agreement. The provisions of section 210 shall be applicable in the enforcement of this section.

Information as to the Act

(29 U.S.C. 415)

SEC. 105. Every labor organization shall inform its members concerning the provisions of this Act.

APPENDIX B-4

SECTION 2-B OF THE BASIC STEEL CONTRACT

This contract language, which had been in place in steel industry contracts since 1947, sparked the 1959 Steel Strike, which was the largest in U.S. history. The steel companies wanted to eliminate the language that they thought severely restricted their ability to reorganize the work process. The union was successful in keeping the language, but the strike led steel consumers to increase their use of imported steel.

Section 2-B

Section 2 – Scope of the Agreement

B. Local Working Conditions

The term "local working conditions" as used herein means specific practices or customs which reflect detailed application of the subject matter within the scope of wages, hours of work, or other conditions of employment, and includes local agreements, written and oral, on such matters. It is recognized that it is impracticable to set forth in this Agreement all of these working conditions, which are of a local nature only, or to state specifically in this Agreement which of these matters should be changed or eliminated. The following provisions provide general principles and procedures that explain the status of these matters and furnish necessary guideposts for the parties hereto and the Board of Arbitration.

1. It is recognized that an employee does not have the right to have a local working condition established, in any given situation or plant where such condition has not existed, during the term of this Agreement, or to have an existing local working condition changed or eliminated, except to the extent necessary to require the application of a specific provision of this Agreement.

2. In no case shall local working conditions be effective to deprive any employee of rights under this Agreement. Should any employee believe that a local working condition is depriving him of the benefits of this Agreement, he shall have recourse to the grievance procedure and arbitration, if necessary, to require the local working condition to be changed or eliminated to provide the benefits of this Agreement.

3. Should there be any local working conditions in effect that provide benefits that are in excess of or in addition to the benefits established by this Agreement, they shall remain in effect for the term of this Agreement, except as they are changed or eliminated by mutual agreement or in accordance with Paragraph 4 below.

4. The Company shall have the right to change or eliminate any local working condition if, as the result of action taken by Management under Section 3 – Management, the basis for the existence of the local working condition is changed or eliminated, thereby making it unnecessary to continue such local working condition; provided, however, that when such change or elimination is made by the Company any affected employee shall have recourse to the grievance procedure and arbitration, if necessary, to have the Company justify its action.

5. No local working condition shall hereafter be established or agreed to that changes or modifies any of the provisions of this Agreement. In the event such a local working condition is established or agreed to, it shall not be enforceable to the extent that it is inconsistent with or goes beyond the provisions of this Agreement, except as it is approved by an International Officer of the Union and the Industrial Relations Executive of the Company.

Chapter Reference Material

Chapter 1
Steel Comes to Chicago

Freeman, Joshua; *Behemoth: A History of the Factory and the Making of the Modern World*; 2018.

Kelly, Jack; *The Edge of Anarchy: The Railroad Barons, The Gilded Age, and The Greatest Uprising in America;* 2018.

Kahan, Paul; *The Homestead Strike: Labor, Violence, and American Industry;* 2014.

Loomis, Erik; *A History of America in Ten Strikes;* 2018.

Standiford, Les; *Meet You in Hell: Andrew Carnegie, Henry Clay Frick, and the Bitter Partnership That Transformed America;* 2005.

Online:

https://www.frick.org/about/history/henry_clay_frick

https://www.pbs.org/wgbh/americanexperience/features/goldman-henry-clay-frick-1849-1919/

https://www.pbs.org/wgbh/americanexperience/features/goldman-alexander-sasha-berkman-1870-1936/

http://www.lib.berkeley.edu/goldman/pdfs/Anarchy'sDen_GoldmanSuspectedintheFrickAssassinationAttempt.pdf

https://aflcio.org/about/history/labor-history-events/1892-homestead-strike

https://www.libraries.psu.edu/findingaids/1865.htm

Chapter 2
The Union is Forged

Brody, David; *Steelworkers in America: The Nonunion Era;* 1960.

Dickerson, Dennis; *Out of the Crucible: Black Steelworkers in Western Pennsylvania, 1985-1980;* 1986.

Foster, William Z.; *The Great Steel Strike and Its Lessons: The Steel Strike of 1919, Its Causes and the Labor Unions Involved;* 1920.

Nelson, Doug; *Labor Battleground: The Streets of Chicago;* 1996.

Olds, Marshall; *Analysis of the Interchurch World Movement Report on the Steel Strike;* 1922.

Sandler, Martin; *1919: The Year That Changed America;* 2019.

Clark, Paul; Gottlieb, Peter; and Kennedy, Donald editors; *Forging A Union of Steel: Philip Murray, SWOC, and the United Steelworkers;* 1987.

Hogan, John; *The 1937 Chicago Steel Strike: Blood on the Prairie*; 2014.

McDonald, David; *Union Man: The Life of a Labor Statesman*; 1969.

White, Ahmed; *The Last Great Strike: Little Steel, The CIO, and the Struggle For Labor Rights in New Deal America*; 2016.

Online:

https://en.wikipedia.org/wiki/Red_Summer

http://ohiohistorycentral.org/w/Great_Steel_Strike_of_1919

Boeckel, R. M. (1936). Labor relations in the steel industry. *Editorial research reports 1936* (Vol. II). Washington, DC: CQ Press. Retrieved from http://library.cqpress.com/cqresearcher/cqresrre1936071400

https://en.wikipedia.org/wiki/Steel_strike_of_1919

https://en.wikipedia.org/wiki/William_Z._Foster

https://en.wikipedia.org/wiki/U.S._Steel_recognition_strike_of_1901

https://en.wikipedia.org/wiki/Steel_Workers_Organizing_Committee

https://www.encyclopedia.com/economics/encyclopedias-almanacs-transcripts-and-maps/steel-workers-organizing-committee-swoc

http://laborpress.org/february-labor-history-john-l-lewis-throws-the-punch-felt-round-the-world/

https://aflcio.org/about/history/labor-history-people/john-lewis

https://en.wikipedia.org/wiki/Congress_of_Industrial_Organizations

http://www.illinoislaborhistory.org/labor-history-articles/memorial-day-massacre

https://www.youtube.com/watch?v=-Q3RUGLfFv0(Film of the Memorial Day Massacre 1937)

https://www.trussel.com/hf/memorial.htm

https://www.u-s-history.com/pages/h1625.html

https://www.usw.org/union/history

https://explorepahistory.com/hmarker.php?markerId=1-A-246

Chapter 3
Fighting to Preserve Gains

Clark, Paul; Gottlieb, Peter; and Kennedy, Donald editors; *Forging A Union of Steel: Philip Murray, SWOC, and the United Steelworkers;* 1987.

Dickerson, Dennis; *Out of the Crucible: Black Steelworkers in Western Pennsylvania, 1985-1980;* 1986.

Herling, John; *Right to Challenge: People and Power in the Steelworkers Union*; 1972.

Mangum, Garth and McNabb, R. Scott; *The Rise, Fall, and Replacement of Industrywide Bargaining in the Basic Steel Industry*; 1997.

McDonald, David; *Union Man: The Life of a Labor Statesman*; 1969.

Metzgar, Jack; *Striking Steel: Solidarity Remembered*; 2000.

Online:

https://en.wikipedia.org/wiki/Taft%E2%80%93Hartley_Act

https://www.trumanlibrary.gov/education/presidential-inquiries/steel-strike-1952

https://en.wikipedia.org/wiki/1952_steel_strike

https://en.wikipedia.org/wiki/David_J._McDonald

https://en.wikipedia.org/wiki/Steel_strike_of_1959

Chapter 4
Union Democracy Fires Break Out

Brenner, Aaron; Brenner, Robert; and Winslow, Cal Editors; *Rebel Rank and File: Labor Militancy And Revolt From Below During The Long 1970s*; 2010.

Cowie, Jefferson; *Stayin' Alive: The 1970s And The Last Days Of The Working Class*; 2010.

Herling, John; *Right to Challenge: People and Power in the Steelworkers Union*; 1972.

James, Edgar; *Sadlowski and the Steelworkers: Notes for Next Time; Working Papers*, Spring 1977.

Kelley, Ken; *Penthouse* magazine interview with Edward Sadlowski; January, 1977.

Klein, Joe; *Eddie Sadlowski: Old-Fashioned Hero of the New Working Class; Rolling Stone*; December 18, 1975.

Kotlowitz, Alex; *Never A City So Real: A Walk In Chicago*; 2004.

Lane, James B. and Olszanski, Mike, Co-Editors; *Steel Shavings: Steelworkers Fight Back: Inland's Local Union 1010 and the Sadlowski/Balanoff Campaigns: Rank and File Insurgency in the Calumet Region during the 1970s*; Volume 30, 2000.

McDonald, David; *Union Man: The Life of a Labor Statesman*; 1969.

Nelson, Doug; Interview with USW Local 1657 President Bill Alexander; April 18, 2019.

Nelson, Doug; Interview with USW Local 65 official Mark Collins; September 6, 2019.

Nelson, Doug; Interview with Sadlowski campaign manager Edgar James; September 15, 2019.

Nelson, Doug; Interview with William Kornblum; September 7, 2019.

Nelson, Doug; Interview with USW District 31 Director Jack Parton; February 24, 2019, and September 20, 2025.

Nelson, Doug; Interviews with USW Local 1010 official Joe Rodriguez; August 28, 2019.

Nelson, Doug; Interview with USW Local 65 official Lupe Valdez; September 6, 2019.

Nelson, Doug; *Labor Battleground: The Streets of Chicago;* 1996.

Nyden, Phillip W.; *Steelworkers Rank-and-File: The Political Economy of a Union Reform Movement*; 1984.

Terkel, Studs; *Interview with Edward and Marlene Sadlowski*; WFMT Radio, November 18, 1974.

Online:

https://en.wikipedia.org/wiki/Iorwith_Wilbur_Abel

https://en.wikipedia.org/wiki/Edward_Sadlowski

Chapter 5
New Challenges and New Directions

Mangum, Garth, and McNabb, R. Scott; *The Rise, Fall, and Replacement of Industrywide Bargaining in the Basic Steel Industry*; 1997.

Nelson, Doug, and O'Day Peter; *Workplace 2000: Participation, Self-Management and Work Force Productivity*; 1989.

Williams, Lynn; *One Day Longer: A Memoir*; 2011.

General

Bensman, David, and Lynch, Roberta; *Rusted Dreams: Hard Times in a Steel Community*; 1988.

Hoerr, John; *And The Wolf Finally Came: The Decline of the American Steel Industry*; 1988.

Kornblum, William; *Blue Collar Community*; 1974.

Spencer, Charles; *Blue Collar: An Internal Examination of the Workplace*; 1977.

Strohmeyer, John; *Crisis in Bethlehem: Big Steel's Struggle to Survive*; 1986.

Various contributors; *The Heat: Steelworker Lives & Legends*; 2003.

About the Author

Doug Nelson

Doug Nelson worked at Chicago's Republic Steel plant, one of the largest steel mills in Illinois. The members elected him to be USWA Local 1033's Chairman of the union's Grievance Committee for almost nine years. While active in the Steelworkers Union, Nelson participated in Ed Sadlowski's campaigns for District Director and International President. Nelson was also active in Jack Parton's campaign for District Director and Lynn Williams's campaign for International President.

When the Republic mill shut down, Nelson became the Chicago area manager for the Illinois Department of Labor's OSHA Division, which was responsible for workplace safety inspections and accident investigations. Later, Nelson received his law degree from Arizona State University in Tempe, AZ, and practiced criminal law. Nelson now works with the Calumet Area Industrial Commission on federal workforce training grants.

Nelson currently helps run the Steelworkers History Project, a non-profit 501(c)(3) organization that promotes steelworker history in the Chicago-Gary area.

Doug Nelson's previous books are *Forged in Fire: The Story of the United Steelworkers Union*; *Workplace 2000: Participation, Self-Management and Work Force*

Productivity (with Peter O'Day); *Labor Battleground: The Streets of Chicago*; *The Soul of Terror: The Worldwide Conflict between Islamic Terrorism and the Modern World* (with Dimitry Kapustyan) and *Radicals in the Rose City: Portland's Revolutionaries 1960-1975* (with Bill Nygren).

The author, Doug Nelson, is reading a report to the delegates at the 1986 International Steelworkers convention in Las Vegas, Nevada.

Index

www.ingramcontent.com/pod-product-compliance
Lightning Source LLC
LaVergne TN
LVHW022036200926
848481LV00003B/704